With best regards,
Elaine Murray Stone
12/8/88

Brevard County

Picture Research by Ron Lindsey
"Partners in Progress" by L.A. Davis

Produced in cooperation with the
Cocoa Beach Area Chamber of Commerce

Windsor Publications, Inc.
Northridge, California

ELAINE MURRAY STONE

BREVARD COUNTY

FROM CAPE OF THE CANES TO SPACE COAST

Caption For Title Page

Windsor Publications, Inc.—History Books Division
Managing Editor: Karen Story
Design Director: Alexander D'Anca

Staff for *Brevard County*
Manuscript Editor: Kevin Taylor
Photo Editors: Lynne Ferguson Chapman, Robin Mastrogeorge
Assistant Manuscript Editor: Jeffrey Reeves
Copy Editor: Lynn Kronzek
Editor, Corporate Biographies: Brenda Berryhill
Production Editor, Corporate Biographies: Thelma Fleischer
Senior Proofreader: Susan J. Muhler
Editorial Assistants: Didier Beauvoir, Kim Kievman, Rebecca Kropp, Michael Nugwynne, Kathy B. Peyser, Pat Pittman, Theresa Solis
Sales Representative, Corporate Biographies: Jerry Thomas
Layout Artist, Corporate Biographies: John T. Wolff
Layout Artist, Editorial: Robaire Ream
Designer: Bradford Boston

Library of Congress Cataloging-in-Publication Data
Stone, Elaine Murray, 1922-
  Brevard County: from Cape of the Canes to space coast/Elaine Murray Stone: picture research by Ron Lindsey: Partners in Progress by L.A. Davis.—1st ed.
    p. 136 cm. 22x28
  "Produced in cooperation with the Cocoa Beach Area Chamber of Commerce."
  Bibliography: p. 131
  Includes index.
  ISBN: 0-89781-277-8
  1. Brevard County (Fla.)—History. 2. Brevard County (Fla.)—Description and travel—Views. 3. Brevard County (Fla.)—Industries. I. Title.
F317.B8S76 1988
975.9'27—dc11   88-22921
                                        CIP

©1988 Windsor Publications, Inc.
All rights reserved
Published 1988
Printed in the United States of America
First Edition

Windsor Publications, Inc.
Elliot Martin, Chairman of the Board
James L. Fish III, Chief Operating Officer

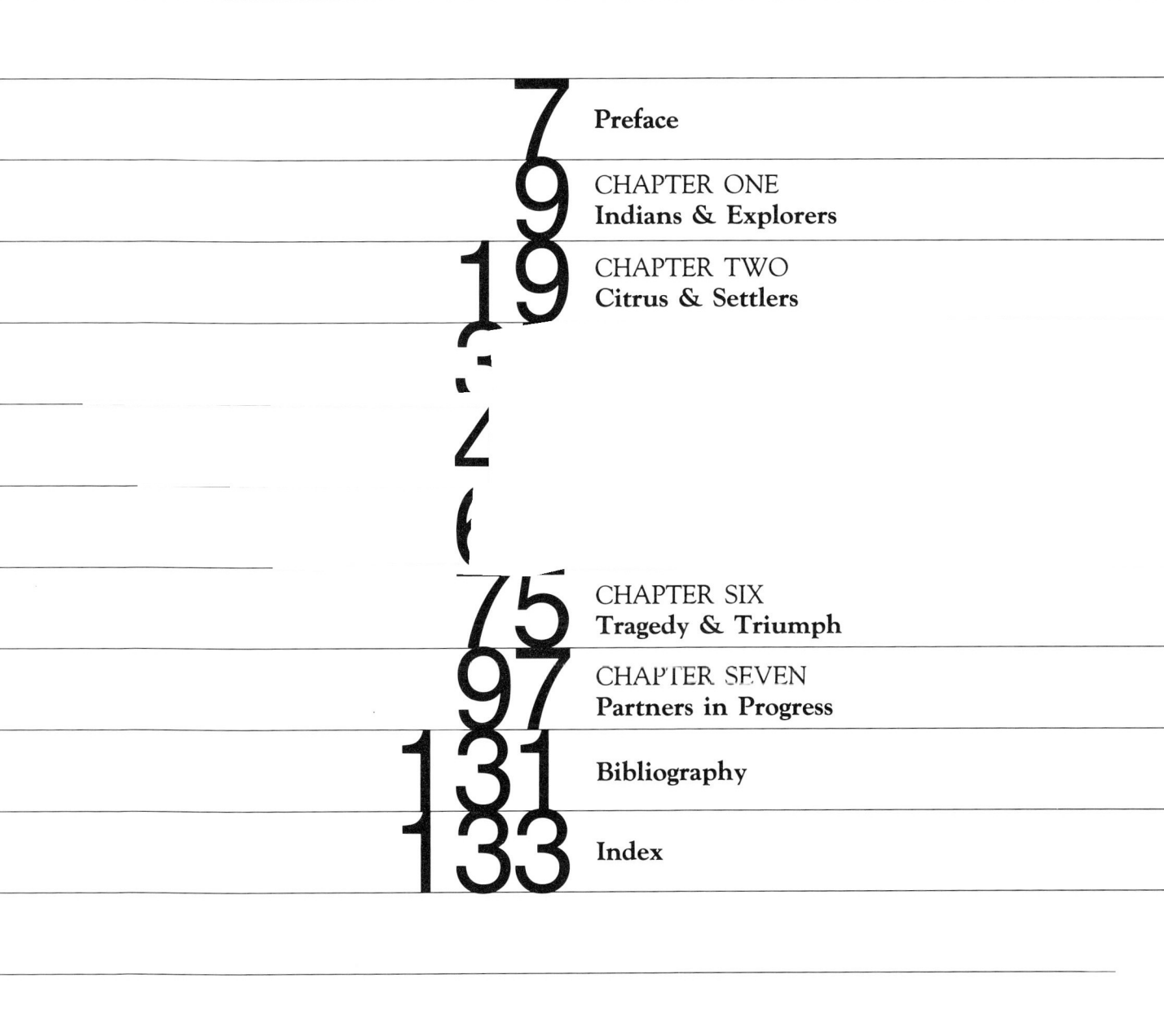

7 Preface

9 CHAPTER ONE
Indians & Explorers

19 CHAPTER TWO
Citrus & Settlers

75 CHAPTER SIX
Tragedy & Triumph

97 CHAPTER SEVEN
Partners in Progress

131 Bibliography

133 Index

The golden waters of the Banana River slowly flow around small, sleepy islands as the sun rises along the coast of Brevard County. Photo by Ed Malles

PREFACE

For the past third of a century, Brevard County has been my home. My late husband, two daughters, and I moved to Eau Gallie in 1955 when Courtney was offered an engineering position with the fledgling space program. At that time Eau Gallie had a population of 900, and everyone knew everybody else. Today Eau Gallie no longer exists, and without moving a yard, I now live in Melbourne, a city of 58,000 people, due to the merging of the cities in 1969. Our third daughter was born in the old Melbourne Hospital on U.S. 1, in 1960.

Our daughters had a wonderful childhood. Life was safe and pleasant, and although there was not much in the way of culture or entertainment, we enjoyed the ocean, the river, and the variety of wildlife around our riverfront home. We spent our leisure hours swimming, sailing, and socializing at the now-defunct Bahama Beach Club and Trade Winds Hotel.

During this same period I had the privilege of being a member of the press corps at Cape Canaveral and covered all the Mercury, Gemini, and Apollo launches. I knew the astronauts and TV anchormen, and participated in all the historic events of those exciting years.

I also arrived here long enough ago to have known many of the pioneers, most of them now deceased. I have witnessed the astounding growth of the area, the new bridges, hotels, and corporations, but have also seen a multitude of historic sites disappear under macadam and concrete, or just rust away in the salt air.

So very much has happened in the communities that comprise Brevard County that I fear some may feel that their family or town did not receive the coverage they anticipated. Brevard has a long history, a long coastline, and many scattered communities of varying sizes. Let me refer any readers who desire more detailed histories of their community to works by Frank Thomas, Georgianna Kjerulff, Eric Caron, Fred Hopwood, Ann Thurm, Jack Horton, and others listed in my bibliography. I could not have completed this book without leaning heavily on the work of those who had already written about their towns.

My thanks go also to those who have written histories of their churches: Amey Hoag, Miriam Hicks, Eleanor Schlatter, Margery Schuster, and Jack Horton, to name a few. I especially want to thank two members of the South Brevard Historical Society, Weona Cleveland and Fred Hopwood, for generously giving of their time to read the first draft, and for sharing their extensive knowledge and personal research material with me.

As much of the book concerns technical matters about the space program, I am grateful to Herbert Illingworth, Public Affairs Officer at Patrick Air Force Base, for reading the manuscript to verify the facts. I also thank my daughter, Catherine Rayburn, for her editorial assistance.

Many local librarians have given of their time in looking up books, names, dates, and events. I particularly thank Elfriede Raedler, Diane Printy, and Ivanka Uhlhorn, all reference librarians with the Brevard County Library System. Last but not least, I want to thank the many public affairs officers of hospitals, clubs, corporations, chambers of commerce, etc., who have provided me both information and publications about their groups.

I particularly need to thank my editor, Kevin Taylor, of Windsor Publications, for his support and encouragement over this past year as the book took form, and Gloria Bloch, who typed the final draft on her word processor, all the while patiently putting up with my constant changes and revisions.

Preparing this history of Brevard County has been a wonderful adventure. I have learned a great deal in the process. I hope that all who read it will gain a deeper understanding and respect for the multitude of pioneers, both in space and on land, who made Brevard the famous place it is today.

Elaine Murray Stone
Melbourne, Florida
May 18, 1988

In 1837 Zachary Taylor and his troops marched south through Brevard County to fight the Seminole warriors at Lake Okeechobee. This engraving by Gilbert & Gihon pictures the last charge of this heated battle, as the Seminoles retreat from the clash with Taylor's troops. Courtesy, Historical Society of Palm Beach County

INDIANS & EXPLORERS

Brevard County has existed under five flags, and been known by several names, among them Mosquito, Orange, Volusia, and St. Lucie counties. The area which eventually became the Space Coast—home of rockets and the Space Shuttle—was once dreaded as the graveyard of ships, to be avoided because of fierce Indians and deadly mosquitoes.

In 1854 Brevard County was named for Judge Theodore Washington Brevard, who served as Florida's state comptroller until 1861. The county comprised 4,390 square miles of mosquito-laden wilderness.

This view of Canaveral National Seashore recalls images of days past, when the land was laden with pristine beauty. Photo by Wendell Metzen/Southern Stock Photos

Initially a real estate development, Windover Farms became a famous archaelogical site in the early 1980s, unearthing many important artifacts, and is most noted for the discovery of preserved human skulls which date back to over 7,000 years ago. Photo by Craig Bailey/Florida Today

The hardy souls who inhabited Brevard were clustered around Titusville and Merritt Island at the north end of the 70-mile-long county. But before white settlers arrived in the area, several thousand Indians lived along the shores of the Indian River, a huge, brackish lagoon between the Mosquito and St. Lucie inlets.

A million years ago Brevard County was a much narrower and shorter spit of land. Fossils found locally contain replicas of 400 or more marine species, including oysters, clams, sand dollars, sea worms, and sponges. Some of these species are now extinct, but the majority still exist, gradually losing ground against the encroachments of civilization.

Archaeological interest in the area was precipitated accidentally. While digging a well on his Malabar Road property in 1927, A.T. Anderson struck a large mastodon bone. Anderson showed this and other specimens from his "dig" to members of the Ceramic Repository of the United States; subsequently mam-

Indians once lived and walked among the lush marshlands of Brevard County, which today are still abundant with life and delightful vistas. Photo by Wendell Metzen/Southern Stock Photos

moth bones, complete skeletons of mastodons, and the fossils of various extinct species were excavated. Other important relics included human bones and Indian pottery.

A more astounding discovery was made in 1982 by Bill Tanner, a backhoe operator in Titusville, when his heavy machine unearthed rocks as large as footballs. Suspecting something unusual, he alighted from his perch and found them to be human skulls!

The site of Tanner's discovery was Windover Farms, a real estate development owned by EKS, Inc. Jim Swan, the developer, ordered construction stopped in the area, and invited scientists from Florida State University to determine the age of the skulls.

Dr. Glenn Doran and Dr. David N. Dickel of the university uncovered more bones and skulls. Due to the preservative quality of the peat bog, tools fashioned from the bones of deer and panther were discovered intact. The thick, oozing mud also had preserved articles made from wood, primitive ceramics, and even woven cloth. Carbon-dating established the bones and artifacts as part of a burial site used by the Indians who inhabited Brevard County more than 7,000 years ago. These Stone Age Indians are labeled "Archaic." They were primarily hunter/gatherers, though advanced enough to make the atlatl, a spear-throwing device that predates the bow and arrow.

Even more astounding, after the scientists carefully pumped and drained the water-filled bog, they found skulls containing perfectly preserved brain matter. This was a historic first, prompting headlines in the *New York Times* and capsules on local and national television. The *London Times* and *National Geographic* sent journalists to Brevard. The brain matter was forwarded to laboratories to be examined and tested by the scientific community.

Large numbers of Indians remained in the area over the centuries, and when the Spaniards arrived in 1565 they named the River of Ais (later renamed the Indian River) after a local tribe. Early settlers marveled at the giant shell mounds they discovered in every part of the county. Sometimes 30 feet tall, these mounds were the middens, or garbage dumps, of the Indians who inhabited Brevard for eons, most likely the extinct Ais. One mound on Cape Canaveral could be seen from 30 miles out to sea and was used as a marker by early sailors.

Another such mound was regularly visited and described by W. Lansing Gleason, grandson of the man who gave Eau Gallie its name. As a boy, Gleason climbed on the mound at the east end of the present Eau Gallie Causeway area (in what is now Indian Harbour Beach). By sifting through the sand and shell refuse, he found fragments of pottery and ancient tools. Deer femurs had been fashioned into knives, tools, and even the hairpins needed to fasten the long tresses worn by both Indian men and women.

As many as 30 to 40 shell mounds of similar size also were discovered on Merritt Island. The artifacts found in these shell mounds provide some information about the lifestyles of the Ais Indians. The Ais retained the shells of oysters, a major dietary staple, for use as spoons, weapons, drinking vessels, and adornments. Shark teeth and stingray barbs were fashioned into weapons. Conch shells that were drilled through, attached to handles, and used as battle clubs have been discovered in the mounds.

Brevard first appeared on a chart, called the Cantino Map, as early as 1502. This distorted rendering of the New World showed a large bump sticking out of the eastern coast of the Florida peninsula. This bump represented Capo de Canaveral, or "Cape of the Wild Canes," named for the marsh grasses that covered the area. It was supposedly named by a Spanish captain, Francisco Cordillo, when he stopped there searching for Indians to enslave. Cordillo and his crew fought a battle with the defiant Ais, who used reeds from the swamps around the Cape for arrows, hardening the tips with fire. The Ais wounded several of the Spaniards, causing them to retreat to their ship. As a consequence, Cordillo named the projection "Cape of the Cane Bearers," or, as it is usually referred to in old books and maps, Cape of the Canes.

John Sparks the Younger, an English sailor, left a description of an Ais village. Sailing under John Hawkins in 1565, he explored the southern shores of North America for England. Driven off course to Cape Canaveral, he reported meeting with strange currents and shoals. Swamps, mangroves, and wild cane fields stretched as far as the eye could see. Sparks noted an Ais village on the lagoon of a wide river. The village contained one big house, using whole trees for the walls and rafters, and palm fronds for the roof. There were no partitions, and the hearth was in the center of the rectangular structure. According to Sparks the Ais slept on the ground along the walls, using blocks of wood as pillows. When the weather was cold the men wore deerskins painted red, yellow, and black. A fire was kept burning all night to repel wolves, bears, and the clouds of mosquitoes.

Besides the British, various galleons of other nations had put ashore at the treacherous Cape for water or to trade with the Indians. Ponce de Leon stopped there in 1513, and, according to his log, anchored off Cape Canaveral with a fleet of three vessels.

In 1562 Jean Ribaut led an expedition of French Huguenots to Florida. Two years later a large contingent of French Huguenot noblemen, adventurers, and families, under the leadership of Rene de Laudonniere, returned to the area they had visited and built Fort Caroline at the mouth of the St. Johns River, near present-day Jacksonville. The Huguenots left their homeland to escape religious persecution and came to the New World to begin a new life and live in peace and freedom.

Learning of the Huguenot mission, however, Philip II, king of Spain, sent an expedition under Admiral Pedro Menendez de Aviles to claim all of Florida for Spain. The king's secondary purpose was to rid the peninsula of the heretical French intruders. In 1565 Menendez and his armada founded St. Augustine, then marched overland to the north, attacked the Huguenot post, and killed almost every inhabitant. In an effort to rescue their countrymen, another group of Frenchmen sailed toward Fort Caroline, but were blown off course and shipwrecked off Cape Canaveral. The survivors salvaged what they could from the wreckage and built a makeshift fort, the first European structure erected on the Cape.

When Menendez learned of the shipwrecked party, he went in pursuit. Finding the survivors holed up in their crude fort, he offered them their lives if they would surrender. Distrustful of the Spanish, half the Frenchmen fled into the swamps and were never heard from again. Those who surrendered were sent safely back to Europe.

Pedro Menendez also led a small force up the St. Johns River, one of the few in America to flow north. The Indians were mostly friendly until Menendez reached the area where the St. Johns narrows into soggy marshlands—today's Brevard County. There the Spanish were attacked by bands of Ais Indians. Menendez felt it best to return to the safety of Fort San Marcos at St. Augustine.

In addition to claiming Florida for the Spanish crown, Menendez believed it his duty to convert the Indians to Catholicism. Accordingly, he requested the recently formed Jesuit Order to send missionaries to Florida. In 1568 four priests and ten lay brothers arrived in St. Augustine. They founded nine missions, but had little success with the Indians. After some of their members were killed by their uncooperative converts, the Jesuits withdrew, but not before they introduced the cultivation of oranges from Spain, and brought pigs and cattle to start farms.

Menendez next invited the Franciscans to work among the Indians. A group of friars arrived in 1573 and began missions throughout Florida that remained active for 100 years. The first churches were built of wood, with palm-thatched roofs. Later missions were made of "tabby," a mash of oyster shells, lime, sand, and seawater. A few were later replaced by more substantial chapels cut from coquina rock. As many as 13,000 Indians were converted and baptized by the industrious friars.

Recollections of the early Spanish and missionary eras can be found in the *Memoirs of the Fontenada d'Escalanta*, as well as in Father Escobedo's *La Florida*. Jacques Le Moyne, one of the few Huguenots to have survived the Spanish onslaught, rendered 48 paintings of Florida Indians.

We also hear of wild Ais in the *Diary of Jonathan Dickinson*. In 1696, Dickinson, a Quaker planter traveling with his family and servants, was shipwrecked off Hobe Sound while sailing from Jamaica to Philadelphia. The local Jeaga Indians helped the survivors retrieve their possessions, but immediately took everything they found—including the clothes off the survivors' backs. After several weeks as a prisoner of the Jeagas, Dickinson prevailed upon the chief to help his family make its way to the Spanish fort at St. Augustine.

Dickinson described his passage through the Cape Canaveral area as the worst of the entire journey. He wrote in his famous diary: "The land, being surrounded by swamp in which grew white mangrove trees, hid the town from the sea. Our extremity was such that the gills and guts of fish, picked from the dung heap was acceptable. We were made to sleep in a nasty place, with many spiders and creeping things."

Most of the party became sick. Dickinson's baby would have died if an Indian woman had not nursed the starving infant. While the Dickinsons were held captive at the Ais village, Christian Indians learned of the family's plight. Sending runners north to St. Augustine, they informed the Spanish governor of the English party shipwrecked and ill at Cape Canaveral. He sent 10 Spanish soldiers to rescue and accompany them to St. Augustine, the only European settlement in Florida. Traveling from one Spanish sentry post to the next, the Dickinsons eventually arrived at St. Augustine in the dead of night. "Had we travelled without a guide," continued Dickinson, "we should have perished."

The hospitable Spanish governor received the shipwrecked party, providing them with food, clothing, and shelter. When they had recovered sufficiently, he sent them to Savannah with a band of soldiers for protection. Arriving safely, they boarded a British vessel bound for Philadelphia.

Statuesque cabbage palms grace the shores of Merritt Island. Photo by Wendell Metzen/Southern Stock Photos

Although Indians, thick palmetto brush, and mosquitoes hindered attempts to settle the land now known as Brevard County, the waters offshore were heavily trafficked. English pirates, Spanish fleets, and French and Dutch cargo vessels sailed up and down the eastern coast of Florida. Typically, ships swung out off Cape Canaveral and into the Gulf Stream, where the current accelerated the long trip across the Atlantic. Due to storms, battles, and shoals, vessels of all types sank or ran aground on Florida's long coast. This turned out to be a bonanza for the Indians, who gathered up the iron implements, guns, cloth, foodstuffs, and treasures. Friars reported seeing Indians wearing nothing but gold medallions and chains around their necks.

On July 31, 1715, one of the worst hurricanes in history surprised and sank an entire Spanish fleet as it sailed just south of Brevard County. Ten galleons foundered in the storm, just south of Sebastian Inlet. When the sun finally shone, the captains of the galleons—fearing for their heads and determined to recover their treasure—set up a temporary village on the beach. They forced the local Ais and Jeaga Indians to work as divers. Using large rocks to weigh them down and empty buckets to give them more time underwater, the Indians searched the sunken vessels and brought up baskets filled with gold discs and pieces of eight. Many divers drowned or were worked to death by the Spaniards.

Following a year of continual diving, a storm shifted the hulks away from shore into deeper water. The wrecks had to be abandoned. In 1964 Kip Wagner and Bob Marx, using modern diving gear and techniques, rediscovered the sunken ships, and most of the remaining treasure was salvaged by the Real Eight Company. Today, after every winter storm, gold coins and silver pieces of eight still wash up onto Brevard and Indian River beaches.

Frequent English advances into Florida—especially raids on St. Augustine by the Georgia-based General Oglethorpe—did much to weaken Spanish rule by 1740. By 1750 Creek Indians, rather than the Spanish governor, controlled most of northern Florida. When the British captured Cuba, Spain willingly traded its faltering and unruly Florida colony for the thriving Caribbean island. In 1763 the handful of aboriginal Indians still alive in St. Augustine sailed with their friars and governor to Cuba. Florida became an English colony.

Following the mass exodus of Spaniards from Florida, many wealthy Englishmen moved into the area from Georgia, South Carolina, and England. They formed large plantations along the shores of the rich St. Johns River.

One contemporary observer, William Bartram, had come to Florida as a boy with his father, John Bartram, the Royal British botanist. They returned to Philadelphia when the family farm on the St. Johns River failed. In 1770 William was commissioned by John Fothergill, a distinguished scientist, to collect the flora and fauna of the southern Florida peninsula for the Philadelphia Museum. The younger Bartram traveled throughout Florida, becoming friendly with the Indians, who called him "Puc-Puggy," or "the Flower Hunter." The Indians Bartram met were members of the Lower Creek tribes, who had moved into the Florida wilderness when settlers forced them from their native areas in the southern and Gulf states. They were called Seminoles, meaning "the wild ones."

After visiting several large cotton and citrus plantations, Bartram set out by canoe for the upper reaches of the St. Johns. In his book *Travels*, he describes the fierce alligators and wolves that stole his meager rations. Bartram stopped to visit isolated trading posts, but on the whole he spent his year in Florida in total isolation, cataloging the tremendous variety of trees, plants, flowers, birds, and wildlife he found in this natural paradise. His book, published in Philadelphia in 1791, did much to interest people in Florida and brought more settlers to the formerly unknown region.

At the time of Bartram's travels, Florida was divided into two separate colonies: East Florida with St. Augustine as its capital, and West Florida, including the panhandle as far west as Mobile, with Pensacola as its headquarters. Each had its own governor and large stone fort, built by slave and Indian labor. These forts had been vital in protecting the valuable Spanish treasure fleets from attack during Spanish rule.

West Florida was plagued by bilious fevers, which decimated the inhabitants of the mosquito-infested lowland areas around the Gulf of Mexico. Malaria, typhoid, yellow fever, typhus, and smallpox—plus various forms of dysentery—eliminated large numbers of the population, rich or poor, free or slave, particularly Indians.

East Florida, which stretched from Jacksonville to the Keys, was considered a healthier area. Doctors in England and the American colonies often prescribed a move to Florida for patients with "weak" lungs. In the section of East Florida that Brevard occupies today, however, poor drainage and marshes bordering the head-

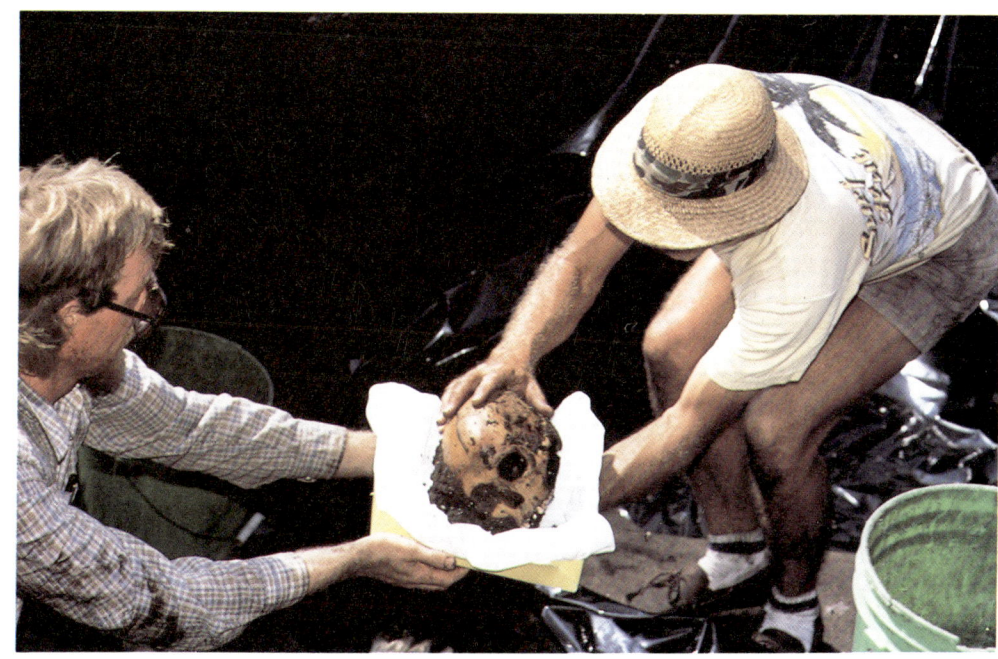

Archaeologists Chris Cujeen (left) and Steve Atkins (right) carefully handle one of the two human skulls which were discovered at the Windover Farms site in the fall of 1986. Photo by Craig Bailey/Florida Today

The 5th Batallion of the "Indian River Brigade" was composed of volunteer Titusville residents. It was formed out of fear that Spain might attack Florida in retaliation for U.S. involvement in Cuba during the Spanish-American War. Courtesy, Bob Hudson

waters of the St. Johns River at Lake Washington created a perfect breeding ground for disease-bearing mosquitoes. This remote area was almost unreachable and avoided by all but the hardiest settlers, a few of whom opened trading posts.

Travel through the central part of East Florida's wilderness was best accomplished by boat, using the St. Johns and its series of connecting lakes down the center of the state. Travel by sea along the coast was preferable.

The first major developer during the English period was Scottish physician Andrew Turnbull. In 1768 he established a settlement of 60,000 acres, stretching from New Smyrna to the northern shore of Cape Canaveral. Preferring seasoned farmers to slaves, Turnbull sailed to Turkey, where he enlisted farmers living in starving conditions under the heel of the Ottoman Empire. Then he sailed to Minorca, recruiting other poor farmers who had lost all in a prolonged drought. Turnbull filled seven ships with 1,500 immigrants, promising them land of their own, tools, goods, and supplies in exchange for seven years of indentured servitude. Upon arrival, the doctor worked these unfortunate recruits beyond human endurance. Indians attacked and burned their miserable huts. Many ran away to St. Augustine, where their descendants live to this day, among them an ancestor of the great American poet, Stephen Vincent Benet.

A few years after Turnbull's experiment, the American Revolution began. Florida was then part of the British empire, and St. Augustine became home to a naval base. The settlement offered supplies, a chance for relaxation, and a semblance of civilization. Social life in St. Augustine was pleasant and active during this brief period of British sovereignty.

A few miles to the north, however, lay the rebellious Southern colonies. Naval activity was quite heavy off the coast of Brevard during the Revolutionary period, and several battles were fought along the St. Johns River. Southern loyalists deserted Georgia and the Carolinas to take refuge in British East Florida.

Surprisingly, the Seminoles sided with the English, who provided them with guns and ammunition. Perhaps because of the Indian's help, the British in Florida were never defeated by any Continental forces. The most southerly battle of the American Revolution took place on May 17, 1777, at Thomas Creek, northwest of Jacksonville. The last naval battle of the war transpired off Cape Canaveral on March 4, 1783. Dr. Harold Gillig, a resident of Titusville, erected a plaque in Jetty Park to commemorate the historical event.

With the successful American triumph over England at Yorktown, the war ended. Part of the treaty included the transfer of East Florida to Spain. During the 20-year period of British rule from 1763 to 1783, new plantations had been cleared, slaves imported to work them, and roads cut through swamp and glade. The English colonists had demonstrated an ability to transform a wild, hostile region into a beautiful and prosperous land.

Upon the resumption of Spanish rule in 1783, most of the British landowners left. Florida's plantations were deserted, trade decreased, and life returned to the paternal style of Spanish government, restricted to the narrowest limits of civilization. Tropical jungle took over the once tilled and abundant fields.

Spain ceded the Florida territories to the United States in 1819. On July 10,

1821, East Florida was delivered by its Spanish governor to Lieutenant Robert Butler of the United States Army. Most of the white citizens were Spanish farmers or traders; the rest of the inhabitants were poor Indians or slaves. In addition, Florida was a haven for both escaped convicts and runaway slaves. At the time of the acquisition of Florida from Spain, there were but 21,000 inhabitants in the entire territory, including both East and West Florida.

During the 1840s the first private steamboats began plying Florida's inland waterways. Stern or sidewheelers, these shallow-draft vessels were able to navigate the St. Johns River south from Jacksonville to Enterprise, on Lake Monroe. Settlers planning to travel beyond Enterprise had to use ox-drawn wagons; horses could not withstand the harsh journey through sticky swampland, amid clouds of bloodsucking mosquitoes.

Although the Seminoles had allied with the British, the increasing number of American settlers pushing into Florida led to tension, bloodshed, and eventually to war. When the United States government broke treaty agreements and transferred entire tribes from their native lands to less desirable Western territories, the Seminoles retaliated by attacking and killing white settlers and burning down their homesteads. These first white American settlers in Florida were a hardy lot of poor, independent farmers and cattlemen, known as "crackers." The name came from the long, snake-like bullwhips they cracked over the heads of their oxen or mule teams, often their only possession of value.

The Seminole Wars brought contingents of the United States Army into the heart of East Florida. A narrow Indian path, which ran along a high ridge west of Titusville, Cocoa, and Melbourne, was cleared and used by the military, and was known as the Hernandez/Capron Trail. Small forts were erected along the trail a day's journey apart from one another, where the soldiers could rest and renew their provisions of food and water.

The Second Seminole War (1835 to 1842) touched Brevard briefly, when in 1837 General Joseph Hernandez (for whom the Hernandez/Capron Trail was named) moved south along the coast, arriving at the "haulover" between Mosquito Lagoon and the Indian River. (In 1845 the Army Corps of Engineers dug a narrow canal connecting Mosquito Lagoon to the Indian River. Before that all boats had to be "hauled" over.) Hernandez left Colonel Benjamin Pierce and his unit at a site where in 1837 they erected a wooden stockade called Fort Ann. Lake Winder, not more than a widening in the upper St. Johns, was the site of Fort Taylor. Fort Christmas was erected west of Titusville.

Zachary Taylor, future president of the United States, led a contingent of American troops down the center of the state. Making their way through what is now Brevard County and heading southwest, the soldiers rested at tiny Fort Taylor on their way to the Battle of Okeechobee. The War Department also established 138 other forts, or posts, throughout the state. These sites included Fort Gatlin (now Orlando), Fort Dallas (now Miami), and forts Pierce and Lauderdale.

The historic Hernandez/Capron Trail, winding through Brevard on the ranches of the Dudas, Platts, and other pioneer families, has been cleared and marked by Boy Scout troops and local chapters of the Daughters of the American Revolution. Quite a few of the markers can still be seen.

After years of fighting the white settlers in Florida the native tribes eventually succumbed to the onslaught of pioneers and progress. These four noble Seminole Indians were photographed by Melville E. Spencer at the Jupiter Lighthouse in 1879. Courtesy, Historical Society of Palm Beach County

Dr. Arthur McKeown and his family pose for this portrait in front of their home on the banks of the Indian River in 1907. The McKeowns were a prominent and prosperous family during the early years of Rockledge. Courtesy, Al and Bernice Stefurak

CITRUS

Mosquito County, part of which is now Brevard, was formed in 1828. The census of 1830 lists 15 heads of family and a total of 733 people, most of whom were slaves. According to the 1840 census, no white inhabitants lived in Mosquito County other than the military personnel stationed at Fort Pierce and New Smyrna.

In 1842, three years before Florida became a state, the Armed Occupation Act was passed. It provided a quarter section (160 acres) of land to any head of family who filed for and settled on property to the south of the Ocala/Ormond area.

On March 16, 1843, Douglas Dummit (also spelled Dummett), a captain in the Seminole Wars, received a permit for land near Fort Ann in the Haulover area of Merritt Island. Captain Dummit was the son of Thomas Dummit, who had established a plantation near New Smyrna Beach before the wars began. Aware of the transportation improvements and fine growing climate, the younger Dummit planted 1,000 small trees on the island. By 1867 his groves were the largest in the state, with 1,700 trees. Dummit's fruit was packed in barrels protected by layers of Spanish moss, taken by dugout canoe to St. Augustine, and shipped north from there. The success of his groves brought more growers to Merritt Island, and fruit from the Indian River area became known as the finest in America.

Another of the first pioneers to settle in Brevard County was Captain Mills Olcutt Burnham. He first arrived with his wife and children in 1844 at the Ankona settlement near St. Lucie inlet, and later moved to Cape Canaveral, where he had obtained a land grant.

Mills Burnham learned about citrus growing from Douglas Dummit. He cleared sections of his deeded property to plant orange trees and pineapples and build a cabin for his family. Together with Colonel Joseph Marshall, he started a sugar plantation on part of the old Turnbull estate.

Burnham's advertising of the rich soil attracted prospective citrus growers and settlers to Merritt Island. He also is credited with naming the Banana River—the waters between the coastal beaches and Merritt Island—for the banana trees he discovered on its banks.

Other than the plantations, the first settlements in Brevard were Sand Point and LaGrange, clustered at the north end of the county. Sand Point, a spit of land jutting out into the Indian River across from Merritt Island, was an excellent place to build a dock for ships plying the Indian River; for many years the settlement boasted Brevard's only trading post. Its post office, the first south of St. Augustine, was established November 11, 1859, with Shubel G. Luffman serving as the first postmaster. Seminole Indians would come by canoe to trade at Payne's Landing. Dressed in deerskin pants and turbans decorated with feathers, the braves brought pelts of deer, bear, otter, and beaver to trade.

These citrus packinghouse workers prepare crates of fruit for shipment to the north in the 1920s, near the Joe Griggs home on Rockledge Avenue. Courtesy, Al and Bernice Stefurak

Just north of Sand Point was LaGrange, another small community. Early settlers of LaGrange included David Nathaniel Carlile, Lawrence Carlile, Tom Coschutt, E.L. Brady, John Reddick, and John Harrison.

The achievement of statehood on March 3, 1845, brought pioneers to Florida, but it also provoked a political problem. Many of these settlers came from the North, but Florida was admitted to the Union as a "slave" state. At the outbreak of the Civil War, there were only 70,000 people in Florida. They were divided by interests, topography, and wealth. The panhandle west to Mobile was cotton country, and plantation owners there, and along the fertile St. Johns River, depended on slave labor. The remainder of Florida's population was composed of citrus growers, "crackers," runaway slaves, Seminoles, and an occasional escaped convict.

About the only event of consequence in Brevard at the outbreak of the Civil War took place at Cape Canaveral. In 1844 several lighthouses were built by the United States government along the Florida coast, known for centuries as a graveyard of ships. The lighthouse constructed on the Cape was completed in 1849, and in 1853 Captain Burnham became its keeper. It was his duty to see that the lamp was supplied with oil and kept burning each night. Captain Burnham was ordered to "put out that light" by the Confederate Army after the beacon was found to assist Union ships in apprehending Confederate blockade-runners as they slipped out Mosquito Inlet under cover of night. Burnham dismantled the Cape Canaveral lamp, burying its parts in his orange groves. He retrieved them after the armistice.

Although far from the scene of battle, Brevard suffered shortages and privations due to the Union blockade of Florida's 1,200-mile coast. Salt was provided to the Confederate troops from salt works at Sand Point and from the beach area now known as Indialantic.

The end of the tragic Civil War brought an influx of settlers to the area, including many soldiers who were rewarded for their service with deeds of land. Some were paid in "scrip" that could be exchanged for acreage, but it

Colonel Henry T. Titus, the founder of Titusville, was instrumental in the development of North Brevard County. He donated land for public use, built the first hotel in Titusville, and was active in matters of public concern. Courtesy, Bob Hudson

was primarily the Homestead Act of 1862 that brought a new wave of pioneers to Florida.

One of the homesteaders settling in LaGrange was Andrew Feaster, who arrived with his wife and four grown children from South Carolina in 1867. A brother had come even earlier and purchased considerable acreage on what is now Dunn Airport. Nearby families started groves a little to the north in the Mims area. Some of these were the Days, Singletons, Joyners, and Stewarts.

LaGrange had the first church in Brevard. The tiny log building was erected in 1869, and also served as a school and community clubhouse. Sometimes three or four ministers used the pulpit on a single Sunday while each congregation waited its turn. The old building sits beside the pioneer cemetery on Old Dixie Highway just north of LaGrange Road.

In 1867 Colonel Henry T. Titus arrived at Sand Point. Although he was born in New Jersey, the colonel's sympathies lay with the Confederate cause. A tall, forceful personality, he was a soldier of fortune during the outbreaks in Cuba and Nicaragua. At mid-life, Titus was confined to a wheelchair with rheumatoid arthritis and moved to Florida hoping for relief of his painful condition. When he arrived at Sand Point, its population stood at 250, mostly citrus growers. In

Top: This butcher shop was one of the many businesses to be found in the early days of Titusville and is seen here in the late 1880s before refrigeration was developed. Courtesy, Bob Hudson

Bottom: This early excursion train on the Jacksonville, St. Augustine, and Indian River Railway spur began service in 1885, enabling more convenient and comfortable travel from the Sanford area to Titusville. Courtesy, Bob Hudson

March 1869 the colonel's wife, Mary Evalina, and their five children joined him in the partially completed Titus House.

It was also during this period that the Rice family came to Sand Point. The story of how Brevard's county seat came by its name is as follows: Colonel Titus and Captain Clark Rice were playing dominoes. They agreed that whoever won would have the honor of naming the town. The colonel won, and the town's name was permanently changed to Titusville on October 16, 1873.

Titus made a lot of money in citrus growing and donated a good deal of land for the construction of churches, schools, and the county courthouse. This latter agreement came with the stipulation that if the courthouse was ever moved from Titusville, the property would revert to the colonel's successors. The county seat was chosen by vote.

In 1879 there were 343 registered voters in Brevard County. Ballots cast for the county seat to be located at Eau Gallie numbered 39; at Rockledge 39; and at Titusville, 135. Titusville has been the county seat for over 100 years, with the addition of branch courthouses to minimize driving over Brevard's 70-mile length.

The colonel also built Titus House, the first hotel in Titusville. Another early Titusville hotel was the Lund House. The first services of St. Gabriel's Episcopal Church, then called St. John's, were held at the Titus House. As early as April 1869 the second Missionary Bishop of Florida, the Right Reverend John Freeman Young, sent a clergyman to visit Titus and Captain Dummit and ask about starting churches in the Indian River area.

In 1887 construction of a church building was begun on land donated by Mary Titus, then a widow. The following year a beautiful stained glass window depicting the angel Gabriel was placed over the altar. Other windows—made in England and assembled in New York—memorialize the Titus family, the Burnhams, and the Pritchards, all Titusville pioneers. The west window, in memory of Mills Burnham, depicts the Cape Canaveral lighthouse. A gift of $500 from Lucy A. Boardman of New Haven, Connecticut, made the building a reality.

In 1885 the Jacksonville, Tampa, and Key West Railroad extended its service to Titusville. Previously, a journey by hack from Enterprise could take 15 hours. No longer was the uncomfortable trip necessary. That same year a single telegraph line connected St. Augustine to Jupiter, with most of the telegraph keys located in the homes of settlers.

Titusville's first newspaper was the *East Coast Advocate*, published by S.W. Harmon beginning in April 1880. That same year, P.E. Wager bought the *Florida Star* of New Smyrna. William S. Norwood hauled the printing presses by horse and wagon over the narrow sand trail from

New Smyrna to Titusville, and the paper's first issue appeared on September 19. The two newspapers later merged into the *Star-Advocate*, Brevard's oldest continuously published newspaper.

In 1882 the first jail was constructed at a cost of $500. Built of wood, it was only 8 by 10 feet square. The first jailer, a black resident, Andrew Gibson, cooked the inmates' meals in his own kitchen. The first black settler in the Titusville area was Joe Warren, who arrived in 1868. The 1880 census listed 13 blacks.

Captain James Pritchard and William M. Brown are credited with starting Titusville's first bank, the Indian River Bank, in 1888. The Pritchard house, built in 1891, is still a showplace of Titusville. Pritchard's granddaughter, Mary Shuster, has lived in it all her life.

By the end of the 1870s, 21 one-room schools existed in Brevard County. The superintendent paid salaries out of a total budget of $2,500!

Merritt Island was accessible by boat from the Titusville (Sand Point) dock. Its first communities included Courtenay, Georgianna, Indianola, Tropic, Banyan, Brantley, and Lotus.

Thomas Sanders, born in 1841, moved to Merritt Island from Georgia in 1869. He and his wife are buried in the Indianola Cemetery. Other early Merritt Island families were the Porchers, the LaRoches, and the Fields. James LaRoche and his seven sons came to Merritt Island before 1876 and bought large tracts of land, planting orange groves on the north side of the 520 Causeway.

Edward Porcher arrived around the same time, marrying Byrnina Peck of Atlanta. These two families proved instrumental in starting St. Luke's Episcopal Church in Courtenay. The first minister at St. Luke's was the Reverend Stewart Martin, who contributed part of the land. In 1987 St. Luke's celebrated its 108th birthday!

Georgiana grew up south of the present 520 Causeway, which connects Cocoa, Merritt Island, and Cocoa Beach. Situated where the island is half a mile wide,

This view of the developing community of Titusville was taken in 1888 at the corner of Washington Avenue and Julia Street. The Hotel Dixie can be seen the background. Courtesy, Bob Hudson

Though Merritt Island was only accessible by boat in the early years of its development, the construction of the Cocoa-Merritt Island Bridge made traveling to the island convenient. In this 1920 view, Merritt Island can be seen across the expanse of the Indian River. Courtesy, Al and Bernice Stefurak

Facing page, top: Dr. Arthur McKeown and his family were photographed on the porch of their Rockledge home in 1907. Courtesy, Al and Bernice Stefurak

Facing page, bottom: The former ancestral home of the late Miss Myra Williams on Rockledge Drive is a fine example of Brevard County architecture of the early 1900s. This home was later occupied by the Rainwater family. Courtesy, Al and Bernice Stefurak

Below: The riverfront between Cocoa and Rockledge can be seen here as it appeared in the 1920s, dotted with its many docks and piers, in this view looking south toward Rockledge. Courtesy, Al and Bernice Stefurak

Georgiana was particularly well suited for growing citrus fruit and pineapples. One of the first residents was Dr. William Whittfield, a botanist and horticulturist. Charles Magruder and Dell C. Munson were also owners of large citrus groves.

Soon Georgiana boasted 50 families, some of whom established a Methodist church in 1886. Still used for worship, Georgiana Methodist is one of the oldest church buildings in Brevard.

Rockledge, incorporated on August 6, 1887, calls itself Brevard's oldest community. Indeed, it was the county's best-known town before the turn of the century. Rockledge lies halfway between Titusville and Melbourne, and until the railroad arrived, it was reached via steamer from Titusville, or by paddlewheeler up the St. Johns to Rockledge Landing on Lake Poinsett.

One of the first men to settle there was Senator Gardner Hardee, a Civil War veteran of the Ninth Regiment of the Georgia Infantry. He came to Rockledge in the forefront of a parade of pioneers, tourists, and fortune hunters. Starting with a small parcel of land, Hardee parlayed his budding citrus business into extensive groves. Hardee named the new town Rock Ledge for the outcropping of coquina rocks that runs along the Indian River. Later the spelling was changed to Rockledge.

Another early settler of Rockledge was Hiram Smith Williams of Montclair, New Jersey. Hardee and Williams both were primarily responsible for the amazing growth and fame of Rockledge over the years. A particularly articulate man, Williams spoke throughout Florida and wrote about the beauties of the Indian River area for Northern newspapers. He served as the town's first postmaster, then as Brevard County treasurer. He later became the first state senator from the area. Hardee served six years as a Brevard County commissioner, and two years in the state senate.

By 1880 Rockledge had become a favorite winter resort for northerners. It boasted the largest and finest hotels south of St. Augustine: the Indian River Hotel, the Oaks, the Plaza, and the Rockledge. All were in the same general vicinity, on the river near present-day Barton Avenue. Luxurious for their time, each hotel had the wide verandas and wicker rock-

The Hotel Plaza was one of four hotels in Rockledge in the 1920s, when Rockledge boasted more hotels than even Miami. Courtesy, Al and Bernice Stefurak

The luxurious Indian River Hotel was one of the many fine resorts to be found in Brevard County in the 1880s, providing a tranquil oasis for winter guests. Courtesy, Al and Bernice Stefurak

ing chairs so popular with Victorian-era vacationers.

The town's first church was Rockledge Presbyterian, founded in 1877 by five members under Cornelia B. Magruder's leadership. Its new brick sanctuary stands on the site of the original palmetto-log building. A white clapboard church, built across the street in 1953, later was demolished.

Not long after Rockledge was established, a new community was started in 1880 on its northern border. Two brothers, B.C. and C.A. Willard, built a trading post on the western shore of the Indian River that later attracted other entrepreneurs to the area. Some sources refer to this area as Oleander Point, others simply as "The Point." Another tale says the town was first known as "Scrub City." Hardee wanted it to be called "Hardee's Indian River City," a name much too long for a postmark. In 1895 it was incorporated as Cocoa. The first house in Cocoa was built by B.S. Willard. S.F. Travis owned a hardware store which is still in business today at the same location.

How Cocoa came by its name is a quaint story. A group of settlers were in the country store trying to decide on a short name for their soon-to-become-official post office. A black resident, Mrs. James, was inspired by a box of chocolate sitting on a nearby shelf. "Why not call it Cocoa?" she asked. Her suggestion became the official name.

The Cocoa State Bank, the first bank in Brevard and fifth in Florida, was started by Albert Armer Taylor. Taylor came to Florida for his health in 1886 with his wife, Grace Webster Taylor. He opened the bank in 1889. A park, on land where his imposing house once stood, is named for him.

Delannoy Avenue was named for Judge John Delannoy, who developed areas south of Cocoa. In time Cocoa became the largest shipping point for citrus on Florida's east coast. Several of the town's prominent residents formed the Indian River Yacht Club in the 1880s, still at its original location beside the Brevard Hotel.

E.P. Porcher of Cocoa was the inventor of the citrus washing machine. He became very wealthy and built a mansion of coquina rock in Cocoa's downtown section. The two-story house, with tall white columns, was recently restored. In the past 20 years it has been used as a library, police department, and city hall, and it is listed on the National Register of Historic Places.

Cocoa's first doctor, William Leland Hughlett, came in 1885 to be the resident physician at the Indian River Hotel and stayed to marry Nannie, the daughter of J.N. Wilkinson. He also established the Hughlett Drug Company in 1888 with Dr. L.S. Daniel, the first dentist. Dr. Daniel sailed up and down the Indian River fixing teeth, according to his daughter-in-law, Josephine Daniel of Cocoa.

The town's oldest church is St. Mark's Episcopal on Church Street and Delannoy Avenue. Built in 1886 on land donated by Sarah Delannoy, John Delannoy's wife, and Mrs. E.P. Porcher, the building was designed by a local shipbuilder Gabriel Gingras, whose grandson George Gingras lived in the area until his death in 1988.

The first hotel in Cocoa was "The Delmonico," owned by two sisters from England, Mrs. Jarvis and Mrs. L.T. Daniel. It later became known as the "Cocoa House." Two early newspapers were the *Indian River Mirror*, established in 1885 by William Barton Smith, and the *Cocoa/Rockledge News*, owned by R.N. Andrews, who moved from Georgia in 1884.

Although much was happening all over Brevard in the late nineteenth century, the southern part of the county had been settled even before the Civil War. In 1859 John C. Houston came to what was later called Eau Gallie, now Melbourne. He traveled with his sons and 10 slaves from Enterprise, walking along the Hernandez/Capron Trail. Houston homesteaded 80 acres at the confluence of the Indian and Eau Gallie rivers. On arriving at the beautiful, oak-shaded land, he and his slaves constructed a large log cabin, which they finished by 1860. Houston then sent for his wife, Mary Vir-

Once known as Oleander Point, the small settlement of Cocoa developed into a flourishing community. In this 1920 view Cocoa is visible across the Indian River with the Cocoa-Merritt Island Bridge running toward its shore. Courtesy, Al and Bernice Stefurak

The business district of Cocoa was situated along Harrison Street near the corner of Brevard Avenue in the mid-1920s. Looking east toward the end of Harrison Street the first Cocoa-Merritt Island Bridge can be seen in the background. Courtesy, Al and Bernice Stefurak

ginia, who joined him there with the rest of their children. With the aid of his sons and slaves, he grew sugar cane, rice, and vegetables on the cleared acres. The family also built an ox-powered sugar cane mill, and processed salt from a pond on present-day Sunnypoint. Houston named his residence Arlington, for the family home near Jacksonville. A marker now describes this early cabin site and Houston's arrival there.

With the Civil War over and emancipation enacted, life changed for Florida growers. In 1866 the United States government was searching for a place to settle thousands of freed slaves, many of whom were homeless. At that time, William H. Gleason came to Florida to make a report for the War Department on the feasibility of starting a colony of freed slaves there.

Gleason traveled from one end of the state to the other by train, boat, and horse. He returned to Washington to report that it would take too much money to develop the area, and as a consequence the project was dropped. Gleason remained so impressed by the natural beauty and abundance of Florida, however, that he decided to move his family there. They traveled from their home in Wisconsin by train to Jacksonville, and then sailed to Miami aboard a chartered schooner.

Gleason soon became involved in the state's politics, and in 1868 was elected Florida's lieutenant governor. One of his trips took him through John Houston's little community of Arlington. Charmed by the serene beauty of the Indian River, Gleason purchased 16,000 acres at $1.25 each, along with thousands more in the beach area. He platted and recorded his development on the mainland, changing its name from Arlington to Eau Gallie, a combination of the French word *eau* for water, and the Chippewa word *gallie*, meaning rocky.

Plans were contracted between Gleason and the State of Florida to open a school, to be named Florida Agricultural College. Gleason donated 2,000 acres of land in Eau Gallie for that purpose, and the state erected a building consisting of 10 classrooms and administrative offices. The college was completed in 1886 on Pineapple Avenue, but never opened. Instead, it was moved first to Lake City and then to Gainesville, where it eventually became the University of Florida. The 2,000 acres donated by Gleason for the college reverted to him, and the two-story building became the Granada Hotel.

In 1882 the Gleason family moved from Miami to Eau Gallie and took up residence in the former college building while a house was being built for them on Pineapple Avenue. Descendants of William Gleason still live in Brevard.

In 1888 Gleason donated the land on Montreal and Highland for Eau Gallie's first church, First Baptist. It is one of the oldest Baptist churches in central Florida. Both Episcopal and Methodist congregations used this building until theirs were completed, and it was also used as Eau Gallie's first school.

In 1885 two brothers, A.R. and H.U. Hodgson, moved from Canada to Eau Gallie. Soon after, another brother, John E.M. Hodgson, arrived with his wife and two small children, Florence and Kingan. The Hodgson brothers bought several acres near the Eau Gallie River from the Houston family, and built a general store, a boatway, and "Windmill Grove," the family home.

Members of the Hodgson family were instrumental in starting St. John's Episcopal Church on Young Street in Eau Gallie. The church was built in 1897, copied from the one in Como, Canada, the Hodgsons' former home. Other founding members included the Truetlers of Chicago, Charles and Mary Taylor, and the John Aspinwalls of Newburgh, New York.

The post-Civil War period brought many new settlers to Brevard. The 1860 census showed a population of only 260, but by 1870 the figure had risen to 1,211. In the Florida of the 1870s, pioneers were like one large family, helping each other and sharing what they had. One old-timer stated, "You could tell a man miles before he reached the dock by the cut of his sails or the rig of his boat." A visit from any other family was a rare treat.

Land was plentiful in Florida. The Homestead Act of 1862 awarded 160 acres of land to any person who paid a fee, built a homestead, and cultivated the land for

This Florida farmer, transported by a mule-drawn wagon, was one of the many settlers to come to Melbourne in the 1890s. Courtesy, Sterling Photo

five years. Following the Emancipation Act many owners gave land or money to their former slaves to start new lives. The first settlers to arrive in the Melbourne area were Peter Wright, Wright Brothers, and Balaam Allen, black freedmen who settled the area around Crane Creek. Peter Wright settled on the north side of the creek, where he built a house for his family in the area eventually to become downtown Melbourne. Wright was the first U.S. mail carrier on the Indian River, and lived his last years in Cocoa. Allen and Brothers built cabins on the south side of the creek. Brothers was a fruit grower. A park is named for him in South Melbourne.

The first white family arrived in Melbourne from Evanston, Illinois, in May 1877. Richard Goode came to Crane Creek with his Scottish wife, Jessie, and their three small children and built a log cabin near Roxy Lane and Melbourne Avenue. Already camping among the oaks and palms along Crane Creek was an Englishman, Thomas Mason, who bought some property from Wright.

Cornthwaite John Hector, credited with being Melbourne's founder, was next to arrive. Also an Englishman, Hector had been raised by a stern Anglican bishop who took the youngster with him to Australia. Upon arrival in Brevard, Hector purchased a small island at the mouth of Crane Creek from Wright.

Cornthwaite John Hector, known as the founder of Melbourne, arrived in Brevard County from Australia in the late 1870s. He established the first Melbourne post office and served as its first postmaster. This portrait of Hector was taken in 1880. Courtesy, Sterling Photo

John Hector stayed with the Goode family while a store with second-floor boarding rooms was built on his property. In 1880 the store opened and Hector was granted a permit to operate a post office there. All that remained to make it official was a name for the new community. The name was chosen by drawing straws. Jessie Goode won the draw and called the town Melbourne in honor of Hector, who had come from Melbourne, Australia. Hector was appointed Melbourne's first postmaster. Richard Goode later held the post, and also served as mayor.

Top: The first Melbourne Public Library was located on Strawbridge Avenue. Courtesy, Sterling Photo

Bottom: In the 1890s a horse-drawn carriage moves along what is known today as New Haven Avenue in Melbourne. It is still a major east-west artery in the city. Courtesy, Sterling Photo

Melbourne's main street grew up along the river on what is still called Front Street. The business district, composed entirely of wooden structures (some of them with docks reaching into the river), was often underwater during hurricanes and northeasters. The first homes were clustered along the bluff area overlooking the river and along Crane Creek. After a fire on Front Street in 1919, Melbourne's main street was moved to New Haven Avenue.

Melbourne's first mayor was Charles F. Campbell, elected with 27 votes in 1888. By then Richard and Jessie Goode had built the town's only hotel, known as the Goode House. It had 12 rooms and was located on Melbourne Avenue and Orange Court. Overlooking Melbourne's picturesque harbor, the Goode House became a favorite wintering place for Northerners. It was also a congenial site for local get-togethers.

The first church services were held in the hotel's dining room by the Episcopal Missionary Bishop of Florida, the Right Reverend John Freeland Young, who made pastoral visits to Indian River County. This was the beginning of one of Melbourne's oldest churches, Holy Trinity Episcopal.

In 1885 Lucy H. Boardman, who also donated the funds for St. Gabriel's in Titusville and St. Mark's in Cocoa, came to Melbourne for a visit. She purchased 92 acres from Wright Brothers on the south side of Crane Creek for the church site, and later added $1,000 to build the sanctuary. Gabriel Gingras, who built St. Mark's in Cocoa, helped construct Melbourne's new Episcopal church.

Holy Trinity's first service was held on December 27, 1886, with the famed theologian, Dr. William P. DuBose of Suwannee, officiating. Most of the services in Florida's pioneer churches were conducted by prominent clergy who came south for the winter. The rest of the year the churches were closed, or morning and evening prayer services were led by lay readers.

Parishioners came by boat to services at Holy Trinity until a bridge was built across Crane Creek. In 1895 the building was dismantled, moved by barge across the creek, and reassembled at a triangular site at U.S. 1 and Fee Avenue on land donated by W.T. Wells.

Holy Trinity remained there until 1959 when a new, larger sanctuary was erected on Strawbridge Avenue. In 1963 the historic, original wood and stucco structure was moved at a cost of $5,000 to rest beside the newer church. It now serves as a chapel for weddings and midweek services.

Melbourne's second church was the First Methodist, built in 1887 on New Haven Avenue. The third was the Congregational church on U.S. 1 and Strawbridge Avenue. The Methodists moved to a much larger sanctuary during the Great Depression, but the Congregational members (now United Church of Christ) still worship in their historic building.

The entire population of Melbourne gathered for this group portrait on February 22, 1896. Courtesy, Sterling Photo

Since religion played an important role in the lives of Brevard County residents, many churches of varying faiths were built and religious holidays were recognized and celebrated. This 1900 photograph of a parlor during the Christmas season illustrates the festivity of the holiday. At that time, candles were still used to light the tree. Courtesy, Al and Bernice Stefurak

Catholics first assembled in 1881 at the home of Gabriel Gingras. Father O'Boyle, pastor of St. Paul's in Daytona, made periodic visits to the Cape area beginning in 1880. He would travel along the beach on horseback as far as Fort Pierce.

In 1904 Father Michael J. Curley was designated pastor of all east coast missions. Riding the East Coast Railway to the towns, he then went by bicycle to the various parishes. In 1907 Rockledge Catholics built St. Mary's Church. That little, white clapboard church still stands in its original location on Barton Avenue. A few blocks away stands the large church and school built during the space boom of the 1960s.

Top: This striking view of Crane Creek was taken in the 1890s from the grounds of the Bellevue Hotel in Melbourne. The Bellevue was only one of the numerous hotels built in Brevard County which attracted tourists to sunny Florida. Courtesy, Sterling Photo

Bottom: Sailboating on the Indian River was a popular pastime for area residents and winter visitors alike, as seen here in this 1920s photograph. Courtesy, Al and Bernice Stefurak

The first doctor to practice in Melbourne was William Fee. Dr. Fee was also a founder of Melbourne's First Methodist Church, and Fee Avenue is named for him.

In 1883 Major Cyrus E. Graves, a retired Union veteran, sailed into Melbourne harbor. Impressed by the beauty of the Indian River, Graves decided to remain. He bought 400 acres on the uninhabited peninsula across from Melbourne at the bargain price of $1.25 an acre. The beachside area soon became known as Melbourne Beach.

Not long after, Captain Alfred Wilcox arrived from Boston hoping to make a fortune growing pineapples, an already successful crop on Merritt Island. He cleared the tropical underbrush and set out 10,000 pineapple slips. Becoming more optimistic about Melbourne Beach, Wilcox purchased an additional 160 acres from Graves in the very heart of the present-day Melbourne Beach. Wilcox reserved one acre in the northwest corner for a park.

To attract more people to the beach area, in 1888 Wilcox contracted to have a pier built on the Indian River at the west end of Ocean Avenue. A narrow-gauged railroad, with a tramcar, transported passengers from the river to the ocean. Wilcox added a bathhouse so swimmers could change their clothes and wash off the salt water before returning home.

A widow and her daughter built a boardinghouse called Myrtle Cottage. The women anticipated earning their living by housing winter visitors in the beach area. Few came, as Melbourne Beach was difficult to reach and inhabited by bears, rattlesnakes, and torturous mosquitoes. In spite of these difficulties, more boardinghouses sprang up on Ocean Avenue, among them the Sunnyrest (until recently the famous restaurant Poor Richard's Inn), built in 1889. Another was the first hotel, Villa Marine, on the corner of Riverside Drive and Ocean Avenue, today restored as an office building.

As there were no other oceanside communities in South Brevard, those wishing to picnic on the Florida dunes came to Melbourne Beach for their outings. Melbourne and Eau Gallie residents could sail their own boats across the river to the Ocean Avenue pier and ride the tram to the beach. Otherwise vacationers and local residents paid 25 cents to board Captain Rufus W. Beaujean's 22-passenger craft, the *Jessie B.*, and later his motorboat, the *Atlantic*. His son, Don, took over the ferry line when he retired.

In Brevard's early days all transportation was by sailboat or paddlewheeler; long docks jutted out into the Indian River at each community. A municipal dock was built on Front Street in Melbourne by the city fathers. Multi-decked steamers arrived every Wednesday and Saturday, bringing mail, cargo, and passengers. Each winter the steamers brought more patrons to the new hotels. In 1887 the Carleton Hotel was built on

These Brevard County residents pause during their afternoon outing at Melbourne Beach in the 1920s. Courtesy, Sterling Photo

the bluff along Strawbridge Avenue, which is named for Emma Strawbridge, the Carleton's owner. Later the Brown Hotel and others were built. Although Melbourne's permanent population numbered only 70, during the winter "season" it swelled to several hundred.

In time, the families and hotel guests crowded along Ocean Avenue in Melbourne Beach felt the need for a place to worship. Graves donated land for the first church with the stipulation that it must be nondenominational. In 1892 the Melbourne Beach Community Chapel was completed at the corner of Ocean Avenue and Pine Street. Services are still held in the original frame building.

On the mainland south of Melbourne, pioneers also were establishing small communities. One settlement was named Tillman (later renamed Palm Bay) after John Tillman, who settled there and was responsible for draining the wetlands and building the canal that bears his name. Soon there were several houses clustered around the pretty little bay where Turkey Creek empties into the Indian River. The first post office opened in the home of Amelia Valentine in 1879. A one-room school opened in 1889 in a citrus packinghouse, with May Valentine as the teacher.

Although there were no roads connecting the string of little communities on the Indian River, settlers used boats to visit and socialize. Sailing was both a sport and a necessity in pioneer days. Several yacht clubs were formed during that period, perhaps the oldest being the Melbourne Yacht Club founded in 1886. J.F. Bergin served as the first commodore.

Each town had a long pier stretching out into the Indian River, most with stores, trading posts, and marine works nearby. Large steamboats such as the *Star*, the *St. Lucie*, and the *St. Sebastian* plied the river. Their captains blew whistles as they approached each town, and local citizens ran down to the pier to learn the latest news, see who had arrived, and check on their mail and cargo. Steamboat visits were the most exciting event of the week for most Brevard residents until Henry Flagler built his railroad. The arrival of the railroad in the 1890s would end Brevard's isolation forever.

In the late nineteenth century the majestic Hotel Dixie in Titusville was a popular spot for tourists seeking the promise of the sunshine and warmth of Florida. Courtesy, Bob Hudson

TOWNS & TOURISTS

The residents of the little towns edging the Indian River were friendly and contented with their simple lives. They had few luxuries other than the warm, healing sunshine and the area's undisturbed natural beauty. In the 1880s trains were the most promising means of opening up Florida's resources to settlers, developers, and tourists.

The handful of winter visitors who had discovered isolated Brevard County were particularly delighted when the railroad was extended from its former terminus in Enterprise south to Titusville. According

The Titusville Railroad Station, built in 1923, was located at the west end of Pine Street. Courtesy, Bob Hudson

Facing page, top: Rockledge City Councilman Linwood B. Aikens, wearing a jaunty cap, welcomes a winter visitor at the Florida East Coast Railroad Station in Rockledge in the early 1900s. This station later became the Cocoa-Rockledge Railroad Station, serving both communities. Courtesy, Al and Bernice Stefurak

Located north of city hall, the W.P. Giles All Purpose Repair and Bicycle Shop provided a variety of services for the local residents of Titusville in 1915. Today, a service station stands on that spot. Courtesy, Bob Hudson

to the December 23, 1885, issue of the Titusville *Star*, "midst the blowing of whistles, ringing of bells and shouting of people, the last rails of the Atlantic coast, St. John's and Indian River Railroad were put down on the banks of the Indian River." Travelers continuing on to the little communities on Merritt Island, and towns like Rockledge, Eau Gallie, and Melbourne, made the remainder of their voyage aboard steamers.

Oil magnate Henry Morrison Flagler had bigger plans for Florida, however. In 1893 Flagler bought up the small railroads and converted them all to standard gauge, facilitating the transportation of masses of tourists from New York to his Florida hotels. Flagler was planning to construct the world's largest hotel, the "Royal Poinciana," in Palm Beach, but there was no direct train transportation to the elegant hotel. So he drafted plans to continue his railroad south. An army of laborers was needed to build the 1,051-room hotel. Both workers and supplies came via train to Eau Gallie, then on barges down the Indian River to Jupiter, and finally to Palm Beach via the "Celestial Railroad," so-called because all of its stops were named for planets.

By the time the Royal Poinciana was completed in 1894, Flagler had extended his railroad to West Palm Beach. Meanwhile, the invasion of laborers and the continual movement of materials and supplies through Titusville temporarily enlarged the town's population and economy. The county seat became a rowdy town of saloons and makeshift shelters—a Southern copy of the Wild West.

In 1886 the Crystal Ice Company was formed. Not only did it improve home life with the introduction of iceboxes and cool drinks, but it greatly boosted the fishing industry. The ice company's generator also made possible the first use of home electricity. Electric lights were turned on in 1891 as the town switched directly from kerosene lamps to light bulbs.

A source of revenue to the community, as well as a drawing card for the rich and elite, was the Canaveral Club, a hunting club founded by three millionaire Harvard graduates in 1890. By then the sportsmen were able to board trains in New York City and travel straight through to Titusville. Canaveral Club members were prominent Northerners who came in the fall and winter to hunt deer, waterfowl, bear, boar, and, occasionally, cougar. Remains of the club's cement foundation can still be seen beside Launch Pad 39-B, where the Space Shuttle sits so proudly today.

The Florida East Coast Railroad was extended south to Rockledge, arriving on February 27, 1893. Rockledge had the distinction of being the end-of-the-line when Palm Beach was accessible only by boat and the Celestial Railroad. Thus Rockledge gained a reputation as East Florida's premier winter resort. In February 1888 President Grover Cleveland, his cabinet, and an entire entourage visited Rockledge at the invitation of Senator G.S. Hardee.

The Florida East Coast Railway reached Melbourne in 1893, bringing more tourists, residents, and businesses.

That same year, Emmet D. Oslin established the *Melbourne Times*. The first bank was organized by Charles and Arthur Stewart as part of their thriving hardware business and funeral parlor on Front Street.

In 1895 disaster struck Titusville a double blow. The entire downtown section of wooden stores, offices, and packinghouses, as well as the city dock, burned to the ground in a wind-whipped fire. Adding to the destruction, the great freeze of 1895 killed profitable citrus trees. The region's leading families lost everything, and it seemed that Brevard was economically ruined.

Some of the largest citrus owners replanted, while others tore up their dead trees and changed their defunct groves into truck farms. Several new industries had recently been added to those of citrus and tourism, helping to pull the area through. With the new electrically powered ice plants and daily trains, it became possible to ship large quantities of fresh fish and shellfish to the north. In addition, the western pasturelands were drained by both the Tillman and Hopkins canals, and more and more once unusable acreage was taken over for cattle.

Among the earliest Brevard ranchers were the Platts of West Melbourne, the Dudas of Cocoa, and the Hearndons of Micco. The first Platts arrived soon after the end of the Civil War, by way of the Hernandez/Capron Trail. They ranched and acquired holdings as far west as the St. Johns and as far south as Fellsmere.

As the drained marshes west of Melbourne became tillable, they were turned into truck farms to raise out-of-season vegetables for shipment to Northern markets. General produce was almost as profitable as citrus, except during the occasionally severe winter freezes.

In the early years of this century, lumbering became a major industry in Brevard, which was covered with huge stands of yellow slash pine and cypress. George Hop-

Above: Washington Avenue in Titusville is shown here just prior to the Great Fire of 1895, which destroyed many of the buildings located along the avenue. Courtesy, Bob Hudson

Along with other industries, such as tourism, ranching, and lumber, the citrus industry provided a steady source of income for Brevard County. This packinghouse in Cocoa was photographed during World War I. Courtesy, Al and Bernice Stefurak

Brevard County roads were often nearly impassable by automobile. Strewn with rocks and often washed out, these roads were difficult to traverse until the introduction of shell paving in about 1910 improved travel conditions. Courtesy, Al and Bernice Stefurak

kins built a sawmill south of Crane Creek on land once owned by Wright Brothers. He had his own logging train, the Union Cypress Railroad, whose tracks ran from Melbourne to Deer Park, 18 miles west. The rough lumber town of Deer Park was frequently the scene of fights and occasionally of murder. There were boardinghouses, barracks, a commissary, and a school, all owned by the Union Cypress Company.

South of Melbourne in the area of University Boulevard and U.S. 1 stood the town of Hopkins, named for the company's president. Here was the great sawmill that processed the piles of lumber brought from Deer Park; Pineda, at the west end of the present Pineda Causeway in Melbourne, was the site of another lumbering area.

Brevard also had a turpentine industry in the early years of this century. Many stands of tall pines were cut and sapped, then processed in huge vats. The State of Florida maintained a large prison camp in Pineda and used chain gangs to produce lumber and turpentine. When all the pines had been sapped and chopped down, the convicts, in their black and white stripes, were transferred elsewhere.

Meanwhile, the sandy trails meandering through Brevard were improved into shell roads when the first automobiles were introduced into the county around 1908. Ancient Indian mounds were ransacked for their crushed shells, and the first Dixie Highway was laid out along the river between each town. The nine-foot-wide Dixie Highway was completed from Maine to Miami in 1915, although shell pav-

ing remained in Brevard until 1921.

In 1904 the Kentucky Military Institute opened its winter campus in Eau Gallie, near the Eau Gallie River and west of the railroad tracks off Sarno Road. Many of the cadets' parents came south to visit their sons during the winter months and thought so much of the area that they built homes with boathouses on Pineapple Avenue or in the section known as Hyde Park.

Another important drawing card for the area was the Eau Gallie Boat Works. Established in the harbor around 1896, it was known then as Captain Bennett's Storm Proof Yacht Basin. As yachting became a major interest in the Harbor City, a group got together in 1907 to found the Eau Gallie Yacht Club. Among its members were General John B. Castleman, the Rossetters, Alexander Hodgson, the Gleasons, and George F. Patterson, the club's first commodore.

Meanwhile, to the north in Rockledge, Henry Flagler had tried to add more popular riverfront hotels to his Florida empire. In 1908, after making two offers to buy the Rockledge hotels while their owners stood firm in their refusals, Flagler took reprisal. He ordered that workmen be sent to tear up the tracks leading to the hotels. The laborers carried out this task in the middle of the night, and guests awoke the next morning to discover the spur to their hotels had disappeared.

In 1912 Tillman (now Palm Bay) was the site of a different sort of venture. The Indian River Catholic Colony was formed by a corporation to entice farmers of German and Czechoslovakian heritage to come to Florida. The promoters advertised South Brevard as being ideal for various types of agriculture. Drawn by the compelling offer, 105 families moved into the Tillman area. Some discovered that their land was underwater; others were dismayed by the heat, insects, and their inadequate knowledge of Florida soil. Most farms failed. Meanwhile, members of the colony built the first Catholic church in South Brevard, St. Joseph's, on Miller Street in Palm Bay. The original frame structure is still in use.

The city of Titusville paved its first street in 1927, replacing an existing coquina and oyster shell road. The structure in the background is the First Methodist Church which was constructed in 1889 and torn down in 1954. This photograph was taken at the intersection of Main and Palm avenues. Courtesy, Bob Hudson

The Dixie Highway connected the towns of Brevard County and was the main north-south route from Maine to Miami. Pictured here in 1925 this section of the Dixie Highway was known as South Rockledge Drive. Courtesy, Al and Bernice Stefurak

Titusville children are gathered in front of the first Titusville school in this 1888 photograph. The teachers can be seen to the left of the picture. Courtesy, Bob Hudson

The first school in Melbourne was begun in 1883 by John Goode, on his own property. The student body consisted of Richard Goode's three children, other white youngsters, and the children of the black pioneer families around Crane Creek. This treasured "Little Red Schoolhouse" is preserved on the campus of the Florida Institute of Technology.

A two-story frame school opened 11 years later on Highland Avenue in Eau Gallie, where the modern sanctuary of St. Paul's Methodist stands today. W.T. Wells started a small high school in Melbourne as early as 1896. In 1920 a large, two-story school building opened on New Haven Avenue for grades one through twelve. It is presently being restored as a cultural center. Titusville had two schools by 1887.

In pioneer times most music, drama, and entertainment was associated with a person's church or home. From the turn of the century until World War I, the main forms of leisure included hunting, sailing, fishing, community picnics, and church functions. Many cultural activities were purposely scheduled during the winter when tourists also could support and enjoy them. A major event, which drew thousands to the small town, was the annual Washington's Birthday party held in Eau Gallie. Each town also sponsored its own Fourth of July parade, and swimming races drew crowds at the Melbourne Beach Casino.

Silent movies came to Brevard during this period. The Gem, Eau Gallie's first movie house, opened its doors in 1914 on Highland Avenue. The Rossetters owned a theater called the Aerodrome—with a hand-cranked projector—on what is now Eau Gallie Boulevard. According to James Rossetter, Jr., however, the biggest entertainment was watching the old "29" train come in.

Titusville's first movie house opened in 1907, and even Hopkins had its own movie theater. The best known former motion picture theater was the Alladin in downtown Cocoa. This large, ornate emporium opened in 1926, and was recently restored after being closed for decades. It is now called the Cocoa Village Playhouse and is used for plays and concerts.

The Melbourne Band was organized in 1904 and performed in the band shell on Front Street. It was reorganized in

Golfing was a favorite activity in Brevard County in the early 1900s, and a popular location for this sport was the Rockledge Golf & Country Club, pictured here in the 1920s. At that time sand tees were used instead of the current wood or plastic tees. Courtesy, Al and Bernice Stefurak

1950, and today is a large, professional-sounding group. In Titusville the Ellis Wagers opened the second story of their spacious home for use as a local opera house, where the young community met for dances and amateur performances.

Romance, too, was an integral part of the Victorian period. Along the top of the cliffs was "Bluff Walk," a favorite spot for young lovers who entered it through the "Trysting Stairs" on New Haven Avenue. Many Melbourne marriages were the result of a stroll up the Trysting Stairs and along Bluff Walk.

One of the first to own a winter home in Eau Gallie was the Civil War General John B. Castleman of Louisville, Kentucky. He bought a large, clapboard house that still stands at the foot of Young Street and Sunnypoint Drive.

Soon after came Castleman's friend, S. Thruston Ballard, a former lieutenant governor of Kentucky. Near the confluence of Elbow Creek and the Indian River, he built a three-story mansion, a guest house, servants' quarters, a boathouse, and a gazebo amid acres of lush, landscaped gardens. He named the estate "Sunnypoint" in honor of his wife, "Sunny."

The Ballard family made its fortune in the flour and biscuit business.

The Ballards' daughter, Mary, married Dr. David Morton, whose son, Thruston Morton, grew up to become a U.S. senator and chairman of the Republican National Committee. Another son, Rogers Morton, served President Gerald Ford as secretary of commerce.

The Rossetters, another prominent early family, came to Eau Gallie from Jacksonville in 1903. James Wadsworth Rossetter started shipping ice-packed fish to Northern markets aboard his fleet of 30 boats. When automobiles became common, he was appointed the Standard Oil distributor for South Brevard. Rossetter built a beautiful home for his five children at Highland Avenue and Houston Street, a showplace of old Eau Gallie. The first Catholic masses were held there, celebrated by circuit-riding priests, including Father Gabriel, for whom Melbourne's Knights of Columbus Council No. 3746 is named.

Still another famous visitor to Eau Gallie was naturalist Thomas Barbour. Barbour first came as a boy to visit his grandmother at "Walden," her riverfront place on Pineapple Avenue. Because he spent

Participants in the First Casting Tournament of the Melbourne Angler's Club gather for a group picture on March 21, 1929, in Melbourne. Courtesy, Sterling Photo

Residents of Melbourne gather on the "Trysting Stairs" of "Bluff Walk" for an afternoon outing in the early 1900s. Courtesy, Sterling Photo

many winters in Eau Gallie and was concerned about what civilization was doing to the environment, he wrote *That Vanishing Eden*.

Dr. W.J. Creel was the first physician in Eau Gallie. Arriving in 1910 as the railroad doctor, he cared for patients from Cocoa to Fort Pierce. He even made calls by boat to Merritt Island, although most of his sick calls were made in the very first car seen in Eau Gallie.

Sadly, not everyone enjoyed Brevard's many opportunities. Throughout this period, segregation was a fact of life in Florida. Reconstruction was reprehensible to the majority of white Southern residents of the state, and as soon as military rule ended in 1877, Florida passed a code of laws providing for racial segregation.

Signs posted at railroad depots, in waiting rooms, in trains, and on water fountains designated those for "Whites" and others for "Colored." Until the Civil Rights Act, blacks lived in their own separate sections of town—usually on dirt streets, with no city lights, sidewalks, or plumbing. While new schools were built in each Brevard community for white students, blacks were forbidden to attend. Taught by unlicensed teachers in rundown buildings with dusty yards, they used second-hand books and frequently attended classes for only four months a year.

Although William Rufus Brothers attended the "Little Red Schoolhouse" in 1885 with the Goode children, his son, John, who was born in 1907, went to the segregated school on the corner of Lipscomb and Line streets. The first black "upper" school, built in 1930, was called the Melbourne Vocational School. Stone High School, the first to offer black children a secondary school education, didn't open until 1958. The Stone High School band was considered the best in the county and for many years was a high point of every parade.

Enterprising black leaders of each Brevard community raised funds to build their own churches. In Melbourne three black couples met in the 1880s at the home of Wright and Mary Brothers to start the Allen Chapel African Methodist Episcopal Church.

During the early years of this century, many of Brevard's black residents were employed as gardeners, grove workers, fish packers, construction laborers, and household helpers. Several black women—including Mary Brothers, Lydia Duncan, Anneda Harris, and Estella Jackson—served as midwives at a time when doctors were few and far between. They usually earned five dollars per delivery. Some black families owned their own businesses, land, and stores. Stone Funeral Home in Melbourne and Tucker Plumbing are among the most substantial older businesses.

Brevard author Zora Neale Hurston achieved national fame in the 1930s. A graduate of Barnard College and a friend of novelist Fannie Hurst and poet Langston Hughes, she spent her later years living in destitution on Aurora Road in Eau Gallie. Harry Lawrence remains highly respected for his work as president of the South Brevard Civic League, which worked to desegregate schools in the 1950s and 1960s. A park at the juncture of New Haven and Strawbridge avenues in Melbourne is named for him.

With the onset of World War I, many changes came to Brevard County. Unable to travel abroad, tourists visited Florida instead. It was during this period that plans were laid out for the new town of Indialantic-By-The-Sea. In 1915 a Dutchman named Ernest Kouwen-Hoven came to Melbourne from California, accompanied by his wife and children. Although Melbourne was still a small town and U.S. 1 only a rutted shell road, Kouwen-Hoven had great visions for the undeveloped oceanside land across the Indian River. He began to buy up the scrub land, then known as East Melbourne, until he had accumulated a square mile. To this he gave the name Indialantic-By-The-Sea, as it lay between the Indian River and the Atlantic Ocean. Kouwen-Hoven opened a sales office on Front Street, Melbourne's main business section, and began to sell lots, even though there was no access to the town except by boat.

In 1921, as the Florida boom gained momentum, Kouwen-Hoven built the first wooden bridge in South Brevard, a two-lane toll bridge, across the Indian River to connect the mainland with the beach. Today, Melbourne's new high-rise bridge, leading to Indialantic and other beach communities, is named in memory of Ernest Kouwen-Hoven.

Soon after the bridge was completed, Kouwen-Hoven sold it and his other holdings to Herbert R. Earle, who added a large beachfront casino with a pool and boardwalk and, eventually, the Indialantic Hotel. In 1940 the casino and hotel were bought by Karl P. Abbott, who renamed the Indialantic Casino the "Bahama Beach Club," and the large, Spanish-style hotel the "Trade Winds." The Bahama Beach Club and the Trade Winds remained major centers of Brevard social life from the 1920s through the early 1960s. Both have since been demolished.

In 1926 a wooden bridge was built four miles north of Kouwen-Hoven's bridge, connecting Eau Gallie with the beach. While it was under construction, 10 forward-looking investors planned a three-story luxury hotel on the west side of the river beside the new causeway. The graceful, 51-room hotel opened on May 8, 1926, as the Harbor City Hotel.

As the years passed, through depression, the Space Age, and the mushrooming of newer, bigger hotels and motels, the Harbor City changed hands, names (the Oleanders, the Imperial, and the River House), and condition. Today the building stands vacant, its windows looking out on the river through uncurtained, sometimes broken panes. Perhaps the future holds a new role for the once grand centerpiece of Eau Gallie social life.

Not long after the Eau Gallie bridge opened, John Mathers built a bridge connecting the south end of Merritt Island with what today is Indian Harbour Beach. It was completed in June 1927, and it cost Mathers $40,000 out of his own pocket. The toll was 15 cents for a horse and rider to cross, 5 cents for a cow, and 25 cents for a car. Once the bridge was operational, South Tropical Trail came into existence as a marl road winding through the scenic island.

In 1935 Brevard's most famous estate, Hacienda Del Sol, was built on Tropical Trail. The Merritt Island showplace belonged to Mr. and Mrs. W.T. Stewart.

Top: Bus service was available for tourists from Melbourne to the beachside community of Indialantic, as pictured here in the 1920s. Courtesy, Sterling Photo

Bottom: Beach-goers near the Indialantic Casino were encouraged to gather between the guide ropes set out for bathers in 1926. Courtesy, Sterling Photo

For decades, Evelyn Stewart was known as Brevard's most famous hostess. No invitations were more prized than those to her extravagant, glamorous parties.

Although trains had carried the majority of visitors to Brevard in the early years of the century, air travel grew in importance in the late 1920s. Brevardians already had a taste of the adventure of flying following World War I, when barnstormers performed for the small towns along the Indian River, often landing in pastures.

Realizing that the future of transportation was in the air, Melbourne citizens planned an airport. Brevard's first airport was built six miles west of the city, off the Kissimmee Highway (192). Pilots planning to land first buzzed the town to alert the ground crew. Some landed closer to town on the golf course, where an area was designated as a landing strip.

During the Depression, a WPA project provided for the construction of a modern commercial airport between Eau Gallie and Melbourne. The Melbourne Airport opened in 1933, on the 30th anniversary of the first flight by the Wright brothers. The Melbourne Naval Air Station built an improved airport during World War II, and turned it over to the city after the war. The first plane to touch down on the longer runway was Eastern Airlines Flight 166 on January 31, 1953. A small, concrete block terminal replaced the old wooden lean-to used formerly. The majority of commercial air traffic for the past 35 years has come through Melbourne Airport, upgraded to international rank and now handling large jets.

The post-World War I building boom struck all of Brevard. In the Rockledge-Cocoa area former farms and lowlands were transformed into developments, with impressive archways and winding roads. The lots sold easily—some sight unseen—and fine homes were constructed.

Rockledge's old frame hotels were demolished and replaced with steel and concrete ones. Others were remodeled and expanded. Roads were widened and surfaced throughout the county, and the Dixie Highway through Brevard had many tourist courts for weary drivers, offering one-room bungalows with electricity and hot water.

In Rockledge, owners of the new four-story Indian River Hotel put in a swimming pool and featured exhibitions by Gertrude Ederle, an Olympic star and the first woman to swim the English Channel. President Warren D. Harding visited Rockledge during several winters, staying with his sister and brother-in-law, the Clifford B. Klings. He returned aboard the presidential yacht *Pioneer* in 1921. That same year a golf course was built on the fields where Wuesthoff Hospital stands today.

Rockledge's leading booster of property sales during the 1920s was Harry Bourinot, president of the Cocoa-Rockledge Land Company. He and his partner, Gus Edwards, hoped to make Rockledge the "City Supreme." Land once acquired at $1.15 per acre soon sold for up to $2,600 per lot. The two entrepreneurs expected to make millions off these unimproved lots. They also began construction on a hospital, which was never completed.

Somehow things went awry. Although Bourinot's bubble burst, Rockledge continued to grow, though at a slower pace. More roads were surfaced, a fire station built, and fire engines purchased. A new town hall on Barton Avenue replaced the old frame municipal building and school. An annual Orange Festival provided community fun, with a king and queen reigning over it all.

In 1917 Cocoa floated bonds to build a wooden bridge to Merritt Island. It opened to traffic in 1919 at a cost of $75,000 and was the first in Central Brevard. The bridge still did not provide access to the beach. However, something soon took place in Cocoa which would prepare for the birth of Brevard's newest and eventually most famous city, Cocoa Beach.

Cocoa Beach, then known simply as "the peninsula," was settled right after the Civil War by freed slaves. Their former owners procured for them grants for all the land south of Cape Canaveral between the Atlantic and the Banana River. A gigantic hurricane in 1885 created a wall of water that swept over the low-lying beach peninsula. The settlers escaped with nothing but their lives, never to return.

In 1920 Gus Edwards, a Cocoa lawyer and real estate developer, bought the mile of land and sank $300,000 into clearing and leveling the sandy peninsula. Edwards brought laborers from his home state of Georgia to remove the scrub and lay a few shell roads. With advertisements and letters in the *Cocoa Tribune*, plus a great deal of political string-pulling, he finally convinced prominent Cocoa citizens to continue their bridge across the Banana River. The bridge opened on April 19, 1922. The charge to cross was 20 cents per car. For the first time Central Brevard residents and tourists were able to drive to the beach.

A casino and four bungalows already existed at the east end of the Minutemen Causeway where "Coconuts" stands today. Hoping to bring more visitors to the newly accessible beach, Gus Edwards advertised one of its major selling points: two cars could run abreast for 15 miles on the hard, wide beach without getting stuck in the sand. He hoped to compete with Daytona for the famous car races held there annually.

On the following Fourth of July, a celebration attracted thousands of residents from Cocoa, Merritt Island, and as far away as Orlando, who poured across the new bridge to watch auto races on the firm sand of Cocoa Beach. The spectators later celebrated by dancing at the

Facing page, top: Guests of the Hotel Indialantic are shown in front of the stately resort in the 1930s. Courtesy, Sterling Photo

Facing page, center: Swimmers cool off in the Indialantic Casino pool in 1926. The oceanfront structure was a popular gathering spot for tourists, as well as for residents of Brevard County. Courtesy, Sterling Photo

Facing page, bottom: These children gather near the arcade of the west patio of the Tradewinds Hotel in the 1920s. Originally named the Indialantic Hotel, this resort was a favorite spot in Brevard County through the early 1960s. Courtesy, Sterling Photo

Below: This Rockledge home was built in the boom years after World War I. Located on Rockledge Drive it is still a lovely home today. Courtesy, Al and Bernice Stefurak

The Al Trail family and friends picnic at Cocoa Beach in the 1920s when you were able to drive along the beach for miles, as illustrated by the car in the background. Until the early 1970s certain areas of Cocoa Beach were accessible by car. Courtesy, Al and Bernice Stefurak

Photographer Maude E. Trail, who lived in Rockledge from 1907 to 1972, posed for her self-portrait in 1920. She was a prolific photographer, documenting many aspects of life in her images from the Rockledge, Cocoa, and Cocoa Beach areas. Courtesy, Al and Bernice Stefurak

casino and watching fireworks launched over the ocean.

State Road A1A in Cocoa Beach consisted of just a few blocks of shell road from Fourth Street North to Fourth Street South. In 1924 Edwards bought the already existing casino, remodeled it into a 12-room hotel, and added 250 feet of boardwalk. He even purchased a bus to transport possible investors and future residents to look at his holdings on Cocoa Beach. By 1925 his town consisted of the hotel, a filling station, the original four bungalows, and a few new houses. Children from Cocoa Beach had to be transported by bus to Cocoa schools, however, and there was still no electricity or city water.

The city of Cocoa Beach was incorporated June 5, 1924, with three commissioners elected—promoter Edwards, hotel manager R.E. Grabel, and postmaster James A. Haisten, Sr.

Residents of Titusville got their first bridge in 1922, a wooden structure built over seven miles of land and river to Playalinda Beach. Titusville was then, as now, Brevard's county seat, and all real estate and legal matters had to be carried out there. From 1900 until 1917 Titusville maintained a steady growth. A section of the Dixie Highway running through the town was surfaced, connecting Titusville with the towns to the north and south. By World War I there were seven automobiles registered in Titusville.

Dr. J.C. Spell, Titusville's first licensed pharmacist, opened the Banner Drugstore in 1907. An Eastern Star Chapter was formed, with Mrs. C.S. Schuyler serving as the first Worthy Matron. The year 1912 was a boom year for Titusville. Many new buildings were constructed, including a new county courthouse on the corner of Pine and Palm streets, as well as the Duren and the Spell buildings.

In 1911 a three-decked steamer, *The Swan* was put into operation between Jacksonville and West Palm Beach. According to the captain, J.H. Howard, the 185-foot ship accommodated up to 80 passengers and 40 cars. The trip took three days, but was more comfortable and less hazardous than a week on the bumpy shell roads of the Dixie Highway.

Municipal waterworks were completed in time for operation of the new Titusville fire trucks. A volunteer fire fighting group was formed, with G.V. Cooper as its chief. Titusville's new elementary school was dedicated in 1916, and a three-story high school opened that same year. The high school, then considered to be Florida's finest, cost $65,000, a huge sum at that time. There were 15 classrooms on the first two floors, and a gymnasium on the third. A new two-story high school opened in Cocoa in 1920.

But the destructive hurricane of 1926 brought the Florida boom to an abrupt halt. Developments were deserted, unfinished as they stood, while grass grew up through the vacant streets. The boom-and-bust cycles and the deadly hurricane were followed by the stock market crash of 1929. Overnight, millionaires became paupers, forced to give away their yachts and palatial Florida winter homes.

During the long depression that followed, very few could afford the luxury of a Florida vacation. Bonds were called, banks failed, homes and businesses foreclosed. Fine new hotels stood empty throughout Brevard, up for sale with no buyers. Roads fell into disrepair; projects and homes already begun were abandoned. Brevard seemed destined to return to the simple ways of its pioneers.

Older residents still remember those days. With no jobs—and not a glimmer of hope that there would be any soon—many people left the area, hoping to find work in the industrialized North. Those who remained ate what produce they could grow and fished in the rivers and canals.

It was during these difficult years that Brevard got its first hospital. Until 1928 seriously ill patients were transported in a baggage car to the railroad hospital at St. Augustine, or to West Palm Beach. Isaac M. Hay, a young assistant surgeon at the Florida East Coast Hospital in St. Augustine, learned of the plight of sick and injured residents of Brevard. He and his wife, Lucille, opened Melbourne's first hospital in the old Crenshaw Hotel, off U.S. 1 south of Crane Creek.

The small facility had 20 beds and an operating room. Lucille Hay served both as nurse and dietician. One of the first patients was Jack Kriendler, owner of New York's famed "21 Club." He had been injured in an automobile accident while driving to Palm Beach and was taken to the nearest hospital in Melbourne. It saved his life.

Melbourne's other physicians, such as Dr. I.F. Bean and Dr. I.K. Hicks, and Eau Gallie's Dr. Creel, brought their patients to the much-needed hospital. Because of financial difficulties (most people in the depressed area were unable to pay), the small private hospital had to close.

By then Melbourne citizens recognized the need for a municipal hospital. The Brevard Hospital Association met in 1931 to organize a non-profit corporation. In 1937, after five years of planning, the small hospital was ready for patients. Located on U.S. 1, it was given the name Brevard Hospital and designated for the use of all patients in the county.

Not long after, Rockledge also got a hospital. In the 1930s Eugene Wuesthoff, a regular winter visitor, became ill and was treated by Dr. Tom Kenaston, a pioneer doctor in Cocoa-Rockledge. Wuesthoff recovered and left $12,500 in his will for a matching grant to build a much-needed hospital for Rockledge and Cocoa. Father William Hargrave, then rector of St. Mark's Episcopal Church in Cocoa and later a bishop of the Diocese of South Florida, helped to raise the funds when Wuesthoff died in 1940.

The city of Rockledge donated its rundown golf course for the hospital's site. On December 14, 1941, the eight-room hospital opened its doors. In 1952 it was enlarged to 28 beds, at a cost of $125,000. Today, the five-story Wuesthoff Hospital covers 10 acres, has 308 beds, and as a non-profit general facility treated 12,000 people in 1987.

Although Brevard was still a string of small, dispersed towns along the Indian River, the approaching storm clouds of World War II were surprisingly going to bring about a new life and a better economy.

Travel by steamboat was the most comfortable method of transportation before the arrival of the railroad. One of the most famous steamers to ply the waterways of Brevard County was the Swan, pictured here around 1925 with its passengers. Courtesy, Sterling Photo

Titusville residents gather for a group picture in front of the Myers Cottage. The year was 1912 and the group boasted some of Titusville's most prominent citizens. Courtesy, Bob Hudson

The 39-foot-long tactical Matador missile was launched from the Cape Canaveral Air Force Station in 1951. The Cape Canaveral Lighthouse is visible in the distance as the missile soars overhead. Courtesy, Al and Bernice Stefurak

HOT & C

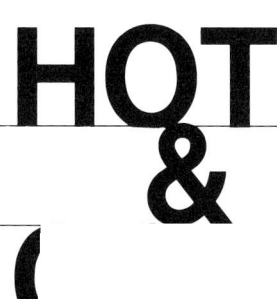

Following a decade of depression, unemployment, and bankruptcies, Brevard County was more than ready for better times. Who might have dreamed that a war—and fear of war—would alter the face of this rural area so completely.

In 1939 Brevard was a county where most residents received their water from foul-smelling sulphur wells. There were no sewer systems in most towns, and Melbourne's telephone directory listed only 47 subscribers! The few tourists came by train or on U.S. 1, a two-lane, tar-based highway that twisted along the

The Old Sulphur water fountain in front of the Rockledge Drive home of the late Myra Williams illustrates the use of sulpher wells in Brevard County before the advent of modern water systems. Courtesy, Al and Bernice Stefurak

Indian River and through the center of the towns. A1A was not yet paved, and the route to Sebastian Inlet from Melbourne Beach was a sand trail. Oceanfront property sold for $15 per front foot, and few zoning regulations existed, so homes of any style and price range sat beside stores, offices, and churches. Roosters crowed in backyards, while the Florida East Coast Special roared through the small communities, reminding residents that more exciting worlds lay at both ends of the tracks—New York and Miami.

That fall, as Hitler invaded the Rhineland, Brevard had its own invasion, one that brought the county its first measure of prosperity. The U.S. Navy selected a strip of land between the Atlantic and the Banana River, three miles south of Cocoa Beach, for a training site. Given the name Banana River Naval Air Station, it would later become Patrick Air Force Base.

Construction of the new facility first provided jobs for local residents and then brought servicemen and their families to Brevard. However, the young trainees had great difficulty finding lodging in an area where no new houses had been built in years. To assist them, the government underwrote construction of Sunset Terrace in old Eau Gallie. Eighty of the simple block houses were built at a total cost of $197,000, with 25 units reserved for black personnel, who found it almost impossible to locate housing in the segregated county.

Celebrations of Independence Day maintained their popularity as the years passed, as pictured here in the late 1930s with a Titusville Fourth of July parade that featured "cowboys" and horse-drawn carriages. Courtesy, Bob Hudson

In October 1942 another wartime facility, the Melbourne Naval Air Station, was commissioned to prepare pilots to fly "Hellcats" launched from U.S. aircraft carriers. Wooden barracks were built for the airmen on a site southwest of the airport. Some of these structures were still in use into the 1960s, and one housed the first classrooms of Brevard Engineering College, now Florida Institute of Technology. Another contained the offices of Radiation, Inc., later to become part of the Harris Corporation.

A few miles south in Valkaria, a replica of the vast deck of an aircraft carrier was laid out by Seabees. Pilots practiced their war duties, taking off from Melbourne Airport and landing their Hellcats on the imaginary deck.

Newspaper accounts of the time reported midair collisions over the ocean and crash landings in the Indian River and in the hammocks and swamps west of town. Funeral services were held almost weekly for the ill-fated flyers.

But all was not danger and grief for the trainees. Local women's clubs, Red Cross chapters, and the USO sponsored dances and other entertainment. A club for those in the armed forces was built at a cost of $15,000 on Front Street in Riverfront Park. During the war 50,000 enlistees used the facility, with the Navy band from the Banana River Training Station supplying music for the dances.

Officers and enlisted men also enjoyed Sunday sailing races, sponsored by the Wildcat Yachting Club. All military personnel enjoyed swimming and sunning at the beach. The officers were given privileges at the Bahama Beach Club, while enlisted men filled the pool and bars at the Melbourne Beach Casino.

Life changed for the civilians, too, as Brevard men enlisted or were drafted. Blackouts were ordered throughout the county, and sirens were installed atop each city hall. All beach areas observed a strict blackout rule; windows facing east were painted black for the duration of the war, with good reason—German U-boats patrolled the Florida coastline throughout World War II. Spotters were trained to staff observation towers and watch for German submarines and torpedoed freighters. Many merchant ships were sunk in full view of sunbathers on the beach.

The bodies of two Swedish sailors washed up on the sand when their freighter was sunk off Indialantic. They are buried in the Melbourne Cemetery on Hibiscus Boulevard. Three ships were torpedoed in one day off Cape Canaveral. The crew of 40 swam to shore, landing at Lansing Beach, south of Cape Canaveral.

Rescue stations dotted the beach at 25-mile intervals, relics from the days of sailing ships. During the war several of these stations were staffed with rescue crews to assist shipwrecked sailors. Today the one remaining station in South Melbourne Beach is a restaurant.

Cocoa Beach became a restricted area because of its proximity to the Banana River Naval Air Station. The beach was blockaded and patrolled by the Coast Guard since sabotage was a constant threat. All cars from the mainland were checked for passengers' authorizations to be near the beach.

The Canaveral lighthouse outlined U-boats in its beams. The prowling German subs sank as many as three ships a night, and the once-beautiful white beaches were blackened by thick oil from torpedoed vessels. As wreckage covered the sand, some residents went beachcombing for useful articles washed up by the waves.

Many of the naval personnel chose to live in Cocoa Beach because it was close to the training station. The small town of 200 or so residents began to grow as new houses were built for the officers. By 1944, 80 homes had been completed, and land had been selected for Cocoa Beach's first place of worship, the Community Chapel, finished in 1948.

Melbourne also experienced sudden growth. By 1943 the number of telephone subscribers had increased to 447, with nearby Eau Gallie boasting 100. Of course, there were many shortages. With 250,000 Floridians serving in various branches of the armed forces, Brevard's greatest deficiency was manpower. The Florida East Coast Railway advertised for railroad workers, saying no age limit or experience was required. One of Brevard's oldest firms, East Coast Lumber, had to close its Eau Gallie store for the duration.

None of these problems prevented Northerners from enjoying Florida's beautiful sunshine and warm winters. Trains jammed with tourists hurtled south toward Miami and Fort Lauderdale, and yachts continued sailing down the Inland Waterway in spite of fuel shortages and other dangers. So many came to Melbourne Harbor that the city had to build more docks for visiting yachts. Because the docks also were used by the Coast Guard, they needed to be overhauled. The entire operation, including asphalt and slate walkways, came to $748!

A small colony of Japanese farmers lived on the outskirts of Eau Gallie, but none were interned. To the contrary, two of the young men served their country valiantly. Sergeant Fred Osaki fought overseas with the 382nd Battalion in the European theater, and Private Henry Y. Osaki was awarded the Bronze Star for heroic achievement in combat.

Captain Alexander John Goode, a descendant of one of the first families to settle in Melbourne, gladly posed for this portrait in 1937 only a few years before the effects of World War II began to alter the face of Brevard County. Courtesy, Babe Kurtz

A popular but unverified legend was that Churchill and Roosevelt held a summit meeting at Neptune Hall, then a beachfront hotel in Indialantic, to plan the D-Day invasion. Churchill allegedly arrived offshore by British submarine.

Recession-plagued Titusville was tentatively selected as the site of a Marine glider base, estimated to cost $5 million, but because there were so many training sites all over Florida already, other states protested. The base was built in Texas instead. North Brevard was not to experience prosperity or growth until NASA decided to locate the Vertical Assembly Building and Apollo launchpads on nearby Merritt Island.

Roads and bridges were of vital importance to Brevard. During the war years, Indialantic's old wooden bridge fell into gross disrepair. Nails popped out of the rotting boards. Cautious drivers carried hammers to pound them down. The toll was rescinded in 1935, but the bridge keeper and his family continued to live in the small wooden structure located near the swinging span. A new bridge was needed, and some pilings were sunk, but due to wartime shortages and lack of funds the new concrete bridge was not completed until 1947.

At Sebastian Inlet, 18 miles south, the U.S. government had closed Brevard's only access to the ocean to prevent U-boats from entering the river. Roy O. Couch, inventor of the Couch dredge and pump, had used his equipment to create a navigable cut at Sebastian in 1916. Following World War II, officers at the Banana River Naval Station approved Couch's request to reopen the inlet, partly because other improvements had paved the way.

The great fishing at Sebastian Inlet would bring prosperity to Indialantic and Melbourne Beach, but initially there were several drawbacks for those early beachside residents: rattlesnakes, no city water, no sewers, and no schools. Children were driven across the river in a rickety bus to schools in Melbourne, and the school bus driver was often prevailed

Many ships, such as this oil tanker, were attacked and sunk by the German submarines which patrolled the waters off the coast of Florida during World War II. Courtesy, Historical Society of Palm Beach County

When this photograph of Cocoa was taken in 1940, Harrison Street had developed into a bustling center of activity providing many services for the local residents. Courtesy, Al and Bernice Stefurak

The quaint town of Titusville is seen here in this postcard illustration from the early 1940s, looking south on Washington Avenue at Main Street. Courtesy, Bob Hudson

upon to pick up and deliver groceries and other items as he made his daily runs.

One of the worst problems on both beach and mainland were the hordes of mosquitoes. In April 1944 Dr. Victor LaMer, an entomologist from Columbia University, arrived in Brevard with six investigators to assess the situation. Brevard was selected as the test site for several new insecticides. Couch suggested that opening the Sebastian Inlet would also help eradicate mosquitoes and reduce the standing water which provided their breeding places. He pointed out that the Indian River was kept stagnant by the blocked inlet, which was bad for fish and wildlife.

Just as these plans came under consideration, a devastating hurricane struck Brevard on October 26, 1944. Roofs were torn off, 50 percent of the citrus was blown from trees, and roads were blocked. The Cocoa Causeway was so seriously damaged that traffic had to be rerouted 18 miles south through Eau Gallie. Schools were closed for days and electricity was out for a week. Hundreds of sailors from the Banana River Naval Station were evacuated to the mainland and housed at the Melbourne Air Station. Damage was estimated at $50 million.

The last few months of the war saw an increase in rationing as supplies became more scarce. The federal Office of Price Administration (OPA) ordered non-rationed meats to be revalued. Five pounds of sugar had to last three months.

World War II finally came to an end on August 14, 1945, with the dropping of the atomic bomb. Both Brevard training stations closed and pilots and technicians mustered out. Many of the veterans never forgot the good times in Brevard and came back 40 years later to retire and enjoy the friendly lifestyle of warm central Florida.

As the little resort towns along the Indian River returned to their normal pace, the Brevard Hospital Service Guild was formed. "Pink Ladies" brought smiles and comfort to the patients. With teas, luncheons, fashion shows, and the popular "Hospital Follies," they raised funds to purchase modern equipment, desperately needed by the small hospital on U.S. 1.

In 1946 a new experiment in living took place west of Melbourne. Called Melbourne Village, it was started by four members of the American Homesteading Foundation of Ohio. After searching for the ideal site, they discovered a heavily wooded series of hammocks filled with many species of birds, wildlife, and plants. The new community was to be owned and operated by the homesteaders, all of them interested in ecology and determined to live off the land and the products of their own labor. The majority of these pioneers were retired college professors, none of whom had previously sullied their hands in the soil.

Founders of Melbourne Village included Dr. Elizabeth Nutting, Virginia Wood, Margaret Huchinson, and Dr. Ralph Borsodi. Borsodi arrived with the concept of starting a university on the premises. Lots sold for $300 per acre, plus a required fee of $300 for membership in the foundation. Melbourne Village's winding streets were designed by Louise Odiorne, also one of the original founders. The first residents built small, simple houses, leaving the landscaping as nature designed it. Most grew produce and fruit, selling it from stands in front of their homes on the honor system—a jar was left out for payment. Residents also tried weaving, silk screening, and beekeeping, though none were successful.

There were many disputes among these strong-willed, single-minded homesteaders, chief among them Borsodi's plan to incorporate a university on the village grounds. Discord led Borsodi to purchase 20 acres on South Country Club Road and apply for a charter to open

Melbourne University in 1952. He had just enough money to erect a two-room cinder block building, consisting of an office and a classroom. Borsodi's university was licensed for postgraduate study only, but with Borsodi as the sole faculty member, few students enrolled.

Melbourne University, however, attracted the attention of the worldwide press when Borsodi invited several leading theologians and philosophers to debate the great issues of the day. Imagine the excitement in Melbourne when the famous Swiss theologian Dr. Paul Tillich, Dr. Joseph Krutch, author Phillip Wylie, and Dr. Willis Nutting of the University of Notre Dame arrived to meet in the little cinder-block building. About 100 members of the press tried to squeeze in with the 78 registered members of the symposium.

The facility and its surrounding grounds later were leased for one dollar a year to Dr. Jerome Keuper's more successful Brevard Engineering College, now the Florida Institute of Technology. Today F.I.T. has a student body of 17,000 from 88 countries on a campus valued in the millions.

Today Melbourne Village is a beautiful community of large, expensive homes set among towering trees. It is completely surrounded by commercial properties except for the lovely Erna Nixon Hammock, named for one of the original homesteaders.

In the postwar years Cocoa Beach did not fare as well. No longer needed, the Banana River Naval Air Station was deactivated on August 1, 1947. After a year of battering by the salty sea air, the military property, worth millions in taxpayer dollars, began to deteriorate. Metal rusted, brick cracked, and nearby local businesses, once supported by navy pilots, closed down.

But things soon changed for the better. During World War II the Germans developed the V-2 rocket and equipped it with a precise guidance system. The Germans used these rockets to terrorize England with pinpointed nightly bombings. Part of the peace treaty required that the German rocket scientists be divided between the United States and Russia. As secretly as possible they were taken first to Texas, then to White Sands, New Mexico, and later to Huntsville, Alabama.

Under close wraps they continued their work in the research and design of guided missiles. What was needed next was an isolated place to test their projects without endangering anyone. Imagine the surprise for all of Brevard when Joe Hendricks made the announcement that the former air station south of Cocoa Beach would be reactivated to become America's first missile testing center! Under the jurisdiction of the U.S. Air Force, the facility reopened in 1948 as Patrick Air Force Base, named in honor of Major General Mason M. Patrick,

Pictured here in its present-day state, Sebastian Inlet at one time was Brevard's only access to the sea. The existence of this inlet has also benefited the ecology of the Indian River by stirring up the still and stagnant waters, which had been a major breeding ground for mosquitoes. Photo by Ed Malles

chief of the Army Air Service Corps from 1921 to 1927.

No sooner had this been announced, and the rusting facility resurrected, than the government purchased eight square miles of dense, uninhabited scrubland on Cape Canaveral. On May 11, 1949, President Harry S. Truman signed Public Law 60, creating the Long-Range Proving Ground. The Space Age was about to begin!

It was a perfect site to launch rockets directly over the ocean, without endangering sparsely inhabited Brevard County. Many of the first workers at the launch facility lived in tents at the Cape, sweltering in the summer heat and fighting off mosquitoes. The 88,000 acres comprising Cape Canaveral had but one surfaced road; the rest were sand trails connecting work, sleep, and launch areas.

Men who wanted to bring their families were hard-pressed to find lodgings. Trailer parks for construction workers and technicians sprang up in Titusville, Cocoa, and Cocoa Beach. Visiting engineers and scientists stayed at the elegant Tradewinds Hotel in Indialantic or the Oleanders in Eau Gallie.

When it appeared that the space race with Russia was here to stay, German and American engineers began building homes in nearby Cocoa Beach. River Isles was the first development, followed by Cocoa Isles, built on fingers of land set on man-made canals. Water had always been a problem for the oceanside city, so in 1947 Cocoa Beach purchased a pipe system from an abandoned military base in North Carolina. This first water system supplied 40 customers with water from Lake Poinsett, west of Cocoa.

July 24, 1950, was a historic day for Cape Canaveral: the first successful launch of the Bumper 8, a combination of a captured German V-2 rocket and a Wac-Corporal second stage. Rocket scientists watched from an old World War II tank, and the old lighthouse served as the tracking tower. A handful of journalists were present, among them veteran space writer Mercer Livermore King, dean of the Cape's press corps. Now in her 80s, she has covered more launches than any other reporter in the world, and still broadcasts daily on her talk show over WWBC, Cocoa.

As America's rockets achieved greater power and accuracy, it became necessary to track them into the south Atlantic. Diplomatic exchanges made possible a series of tracking stations throughout the Bahamas, West Indies, and later as far away as Ascension Island off the coast of Africa.

Brevard experienced a continuing invasion of scientists, technicians, engineers, and reporters to staff these stations and design and launch the missiles and rockets. Throughout the early 1950s all towns in South and Central Brevard experienced instant growth accompanied by grave shortages of everything. Schools built in the 1920s were inadequate and overcrowded. Classes were put on double sessions, and the construction of new schools began. The first motels were built: the Starlite in Cocoa Beach and the Colonial Inn on U.S. 1 in Melbourne.

While the rest of the country suffered a mild recession, rumors spread that Brevard had jobs aplenty in every category. Major corporations bid on government contracts, and the winners offered generous salaries, plus hardship bonuses to those who were willing to relocate to isolated Brevard. Many who came stayed for life. They discovered that Brevard County had a great climate, year-round sports, and was a safe and pleasant place to raise children.

Developers swarmed to the areas with limited housing. Workers who could not find a place to live in the beach towns rented rooms, stayed in hotels, or got on waiting lists for apartments and houses on the mainland. It was a bonanza for builders, but a disaster for overcrowded service industries. In 1954 Brevard Hospital added a new wing, but the halls were still crowded with beds. In Brevard and Wuesthoff hospitals, doctors and visitors weaved their way through corridors filled with patients.

The two-lane road leading up A1A through Patrick Air Force Base and on to the Cape was a nightmare. Even with car pools, workers spent an hour each way riding to work in bumper-to-bumper traffic. All the causeways from the mainland were jammed. Only when Florida Governor Haydon Burns came to tour the booming area and got stuck in traffic on the Eau Gallie Causeway for an hour did he return to Tallahassee and push through funding of a four-lane road.

The Cape, Patrick, and the Island tracking stations were combined in 1958 to form the Air Force Eastern Test Range, a vast missile testing laboratory for the Air Force, Army, Navy, and later, NASA. As the cold war with Russia heated up, more money and staff were dedicated to building intercontinental ballistic missiles with more lethal payloads. Naturally, all personnel had to have "secret clearance" and were instantly fired if caught leaking information to anyone, even their families.

Word rarely filtered out to the public or press prior to a launch, and tourists could not view the facilities. When a ballistic missile such as the Vanguard, Minuteman, or Polaris was launched, workers often did not come home for days, as one delay followed another. Of course when the ground shook and the sky lit up everyone in Brevard knew there had been a launch. Not all tests were successful, however. Several missiles and rockets blew up, spewing deadly fragments over the ocean and sometimes even on Cocoa Beach.

Melbourne, Cocoa, and other mainland towns were bursting at the seams. Many engineers, on moving to Florida, dreamed of owning a home near the ocean. As a result two new towns, Satellite Beach and Indian Harbour Beach, were established.

Percy L. Hedgecock arrived in Brevard in 1951 from Winston-Salem, North Carolina, where he had been a builder. Hearing about the Florida Boom, he scouted first around Dade County as a possible site for a development. But when he saw the beautiful, vast uninhabited area south of Patrick Air Force Base, his heart told him, "This is it." Hedgecock, together with several other landowners, decided to build a city for space industry workers between the Atlantic Ocean and the Banana River. The total area under consideration was two and a half square miles. Mosquito control canals had already been dredged in the shoreline of the Banana River, and eventually became prime waterfront properties.

A contest was held to name the town, and on August 3, 1957, Satellite Beach was declared a new community in Florida. The town had a population of 100, and Hedgecock served as mayor until 1973. Satellite Beach grew rapidly with different priced homes in various developments. To ensure an attractive city, zoning required paved streets and a minimum size of 1,200 square feet for houses. Three new grade schools, a library, civic center, and city hall were built. In 1962 Satellite High School, famous for its high standard of scholarship, opened. Today Satellite Beach is home to 10,000 residents, comprising young families and retirees living in condos, small family homes, and expensive canal-front houses.

Just north of the Eau Gallie Causeway on the Banana River was a mangrove area that had belonged to the pioneer Gleason family. Most of the land was marshy, requiring fill. There was no road leading north on South Patrick Drive, except for a half-mile access to Mather's Bridge. When Indian Harbour Beach was incorporated in 1955, just four houses existed.

Then Lansing Gleason and Charles Nelson began developing the area and building houses. One of the first projects was Harbour Isles, a collection of gracious canal-front houses leading into the Banana River, with direct access to the Indian River. Engineers and doctors who loved sailing bought these houses, where they could keep a large boat at the dock in the backyard.

Ocean Breeze was Indian Harbour Beach's first and only school. Older students are still bused to junior and senior high schools in Satellite Beach or Indialantic.

In 1961 the Gleason family donated three acres on the beautiful Banana River as the new site of the historic Eau Gallie Yacht Club. A lovely clubhouse, pool, tennis courts, and docks complemented the private club, which opened with a huge cocktail party in 1962. The club's location drew more people to Indian Harbour Beach. It also contributed to the closing and later demolition of the Bahama Beach Club and the Trade Winds Club in Indialantic. Their members transferred to the new facility, which promptly became the social center of South Brevard, and remains so to this day.

The Old Cape Canaveral Pier (seen here in 1920) was built by a Mr. Worley, and was eventually burned down by the Cape Canaveral Fire Department in the early 1950s in an effort to prevent the spread of fire. Courtesy, Al and Bernice Stefurak

Indian Harbour Beach residents have their own clubhouse, with a pool and tennis courts, on Banana River Drive. Today there are several major shopping centers in the town, as well as beachfront condominiums and town houses. A new waterfront area also is being developed north of Mather's Bridge. Exclusive South Merritt Island, located a stone's throw away and accessible only via Mather's Bridge or the more recent Pineda Causeway, is considered the most beautiful location in the county. South Merritt Island's estates stretch from the Indian River to the Banana River.

During the 1950s and 1960s the area on Merritt Island around the 520 Causeway began to develop. Stores and restaurants were built, and a few developments started, such as New Found Harbour to the south of the causeway. The First Baptist Church of Merritt Island was founded, which ultimately became the largest church in Brevard.

The dredging and development of central Florida's major ocean access, Port Canaveral, was of great import. Since 1878 pioneer residents of Brevard and Volusia counties had tried to convince the government of the need for a deep water harbor. It was not until 1950 that the U.S. Navy enlarged the port as an auxiliary to its nearby launching sites, planning to use the waterway to transport the giant rockets, which were too large for trucks or trains. In 1951 the first dredges entered the port area and began widening and deepening the natural opening to the sea. Ceremonies—including a water show and two dances—celebrated the opening of the port's 27-foot-deep channel and turning basin on November 24, 1953. Submarines used to launch the Polaris, Poseidon, and Trident ballistic missiles have been berthed there, and tracking vessels such as the U.S.N.S. *Range Sentinel*, *Redstone*, and *Vanguard* make the port their home. Marine recovery ships, used to rescue astronauts and retrieve shuttle boosters from the sea, also are berthed there.

In 1987 more than 2.5 million tons of cargo passed through Port Canaveral. Mid-Florida Freezer/Warehouses are located at the port's main cargo wharf. Mid-Florida's 5.1 million cubic feet of refrigerated storage space gives Port Canaveral more dockside freezer/chill capacity than any other port in the country. The port is also home to two cruise lines. The *Scandinavian Sky*, owned by SeaEscape LTD, sails on daily 12-hour "cruises to nowhere" and on a monthly two-night cruise to Freeport, Bahamas. The *Star/Ship Oceanic* and *Star/Ship Royale*, owned by Premier Cruise Lines, sail on three- and four-night cruises to Nassau, Bahamas, and an out island.

A prolific fishing industry has been established at Port Canaveral. A fleet of 100 commercial fishing vessels operates out of the port and did a wholesale business of $80 million in 1987, making Port Canaveral one of the largest seafood-producing ports in the nation that year.

Port Canaveral is constantly expanding facilities to accommodate their growing business. In 1987 Port Canaveral had an economic impact of $340 million on the east central Florida area. To complement growth the port has also established itself as a foreign trade zone (FTZ).

Port Canaveral has developed into central Florida's primary ocean access. Seen here in its current condition, the port was first dredged in the early 1950s and has expanded to accommodate cruise ships and other large seafaring vessels. Photo by Ed Malles

The FTZ will cater to the high technology field, including the commercialization of space.

A city has grown up around the port called Cape Canaveral. First settled in 1856, it was not incorporated until 1962. Cape Canaveral's 400-foot pier, built in 1961, is a popular place for national fishing and surfing contests. Jetty Park at Port Canaveral was and is a favorite spot to view launches. It instantly became more popular when the National Air and Space Administration (NASA) introduced the seven original astronauts, whose heroic Mercury missions focused world attention on Brevard.

The first historic lunar landing of the Apollo program occurred on July 16, 1969, paving the way for subsequent missions to the moon. This spectacular image was taken during the Apollo 17 mission in 1972, as Commander Eugene A. Cernan saluted the U.S. flag at the Taurus-Littrow landing site. Courtesy, NASA

MISSILES & ROCKETS

The decade from 1960 to 1970 was one of the most exciting in history, when the first man walked on the moon. Not only were the Apollo astronauts Americans, but they also began their great adventure in Brevard County!

Following the U.S.S.R.'s successful launch of Sputnik on October 4, 1957, the space race was on. Unfortunately, America lagged far behind the Russians. Congress quickly voted immense sums to inaugurate the Mercury program. Suddenly, money was available for research to build and test rockets, and most of it was funneled into Brevard County.

Above: Astronaut Alan Shepard blasts off from Cape Canaveral aboard the Mercury-Redstone Rocket in his "Freedom 7" capsule on May 5, 1961. Courtesy, NASA

Above, right: Alan Shepard played a major role in the history of our space programs, from being the first man in space to commanding the Apollo 14 mission. This portrait of Shepard was taken in 1970 for the Apollo program. Courtesy, NASA

Project Mercury was announced to the world in 1958, when seven of our nation's finest test pilots—John Glenn, Scott Carpenter, Gordon Cooper, Virgil "Gus" Grissom, Walter Schirra, Alan Shepard, and Donald "Deke" Slayton—were selected to be the first astronauts. All had military backgrounds, engineering degrees, and were highly motivated and fearless.

These seven men first trained at Langley Air Field, Virginia, close to their homes and families. They also worked at the Navy's Accelerator Laboratory in Johnston, Pennsylvania, and in the centrifuge at Edwards Air Force Base, California.

As the time approached for the first manned mission, all seven moved to the Cape to prepare for the Mercury launch and practice in the flight simulator. Some stayed at quarters on Patrick Air Force Base, others in Cocoa Beach's first motel, the Starlite on A1A.

While preparing for their missions in Brevard, the astronauts were constantly visible to the admiring locals. The seven were regularly seen at Ramon's Restaurant on the 520 Causeway and at Bernard's Surf on Atlantic Avenue (both in Cocoa Beach), or while jogging on the beach, fishing, or waterskiing.

NASA was still designing a safe space suit and testing the Redstone rocket when Russian cosmonaut Yuri Gagarin beat them into space on April 12, 1961. Ham, NASA's test chimp, had already proven the safety of America's system, but several setbacks kept our astronauts on the ground, a great disappointment to American scientists. But delays also added excitement, and each of the seven astronauts hoped to be first in space. Alan Shepard proved to be the lucky one.

A modified Mercury-Redstone was used for America's first successful manned flight. Shepard lifted off from Cape Canaveral on his 15-minute, suborbital flight on May 5, 1961. His "Freedom 7" capsule rose 115 miles into the sky and landed 302 miles downrange, where Navy frogmen rescued it from the Atlantic swells. Returned to the Cape by helicopter, Shepard was examined by a team of doctors and declared fit.

Alan Shepard became an instant hero. Just as quickly, Cocoa Beach became famous as the home of the astronauts. To celebrate the historic event, a local elementary school was renamed "Freedom 7."

With Mission Control located at the Cape, scientists and engineers gravitated to Cocoa Beach, the largest city next to the Cape. Cocoa Beach became the bedroom community for space engineers and the fastest growing city in the county. It also became a mecca for tourists hoping to catch a glimpse of the famous astronauts. Houses, apartments, and motels could not be built fast enough. By 1960 the once tiny town had grown to a population of 3,475. Clubs and civic organizations sprang up like mushrooms. The Surfside Theater was organized, and St. David's By-the-Sea Episcopal Church, a large Methodist church, and shopping strips were built during this period. The city commission had its hands full providing adequate roads, water, and sewer facilities, police and fire protection, and recreational areas.

The second manned mission from Cape Canaveral almost ended in tragedy when Virgil Grissom's capsule turned upside down in the Atlantic Ocean. Finally, all Americans, particularly residents of Brevard County, received a shot of national pride on February 20, 1962, as John Glenn orbited the earth three times in his tiny capsule, "Friendship 7."

That day 75,000 people jammed Cocoa Beach to watch the lift-off of America's first man in space. The 100-room Starlite Motel served as press headquarters for the 500 newsmen and women who covered the historic event. John Glenn became a national hero overnight.

Three days later President John F. Kennedy and Vice President Lyndon B. Johnson welcomed the astronaut back with a hometown parade through Cocoa Beach. Later Glenn was honored at the White House and given the traditional ticker tape parade in New York City. Members of the launch team also honored for their roles included G. Merritt Preston of Indian Harbour Beach, the launch director, and Dr. Kurt Debus of Cocoa Beach, the mission director.

Project Mercury had been designed to demonstrate that man could withstand

Vice President Lyndon Johnson, astronaut John Glenn, Jr., and his wife Annie, greet spectators during the welcome back parade through Cocoa Beach on February 23, 1962. Courtesy, NASA

the acceleration of a rocket launch, prolonged weightlessness, and heat and deceleration at re-entry. The project was a success—no astronaut experienced any ill effects because of a mission. As Mercury launches continued during the early 1960s, hordes of TV crews and photographers descended on Cocoa Beach to cover every aspect of the astronauts' lives: training in the mock-ups, workouts on the handball court, visits with wives and children, and recreation times at motels and restaurants. Walter Cronkite and Chet Huntley were regular anchormen for these events.

Cocoa Beach quickly became the most famous, if not infamous, city in Brevard when David Brinkley made it the target of an NBC television report on October 11, 1961. Arriving with his camera crew, he focused on the seamy side of Cocoa Beach—the raunchy nightclubs, topless bars, and drunks driving recklessly on the beach. Residents reacted with outrage as the town became known to outsiders as "Sin City." Mayor Bob Murkshe raised a storm of protest and citizens showered NBC with letters. Quiet, family-oriented Brevard did not relish the image that had been projected across America. Brinkley failed to mention the high caliber of education, the national science fair winners from local schools, the many churches and community activities, or the Brevard Symphony Orchestra.

It took Cocoa Beach many years to live down the raw reputation earned by that one television program. However, none of this adverse publicity kept sightseers away from Cocoa Beach or other places in Brevard County.

As the space craze continued, entrepreneurs built several motels, including the Howard Johnson's, the Holiday Inn, and the Cape Colony Motel (the latter was sponsored by the astronauts themselves). Wolfie's Restaurant in the Ramada Inn was a favorite spot for the press to gather. When a new city hall was completed in Cocoa Beach, Barbara Eden of the popular TV show "I Dream of Jeannie" visited it. The show was set in Cocoa Beach.

A new 45-bed hospital, the Cape Canaveral Hospital, was built on landfill along the 520 Causeway. Large electronic and aerospace corporations that had contracts with NASA built office buildings in both Cocoa Beach and a little further north in the town of Cape Canaveral. These companies included Boeing, Bendix, Lockheed, Chrysler, and General Electric.

On the northeast border of Patrick Air Field, a giant technical laboratory was under construction for use by the military, Pan American Airways, and RCA. It is still popular to have your photograph taken there, in front of the massive display of rockets.

The Cuban missile crisis almost obliterated news of the successful Mercury missions of Schirra and Carpenter. The U.S. Army sent a number of troops to Patrick Air Force Base and installed tents to house them. Barbed wire encircled the compound and giant Air Force transport planes flew in and out. Hawk and other anti-aircraft missiles on portable launchers were hidden behind the dunes in Satellite Beach. Security was tightened at all entrances to Patrick and the Cape. It was a nerve-racking period for Florida residents.

In 1962 NASA announced Project Gemini, designed to thrust two men into space in a larger capsule using a massive Titan missile as the launch vehicle. NASA also selected another group of nine astronauts. These men began training for the more complex missions, to include space walks and docking with other vehicles.

That same year, South Brevard got its own branch courthouse on Neiman Avenue in Melbourne, with Judge Tom Waddell presiding. A much-needed municipal auditorium was built in Wells Park at a cost of $375,000. Melbourne High School students, under guidance of their principal, Dr. B. Frank Brown, were cited as brilliant future scientists in a five-page story in the *Saturday Evening Post* on December 15, 1962. *Life* and *Time* magazines devoted entire sections to the remarkable school and its famous educator. Dr. Brown inaugurated the Phase System and Advanced Study programs, later copied by schools all over America.

A landmark event occurred on the sunny day of November 17, 1963, when President John F. Kennedy arrived for a tour of the Cape. Followed by a retinue of White House and local press, the president was escorted to the cement blockhouse then used as Mission Control. Inside, Dr. Wernher Von Braun demonstrated his plan for three Americans to go to the moon. Using a plastic mock-up, the scientist explained how the Saturn booster would fire its five giant engines and thrust a three-man Apollo capsule into space on a 250,000-mile trip to the moon.

Five days later Kennedy was assassinated. As a nation mourned the death of its young president, historic Cape Canaveral was renamed Cape Kennedy in his memory. Brevard residents and space employees received another shock when the new president, Lyndon B. Johnson, moved NASA's Mission Control to Houston. This meant billions of dollars that would have been spent in Brevard were diverted to Johnson's home state of Texas. As a consequence all astronauts moved their families to Houston and only arrived at the Cape a few days prior to a launch. Launch Control, however, remained in Brevard.

During the 1960s many new enterprises were begun in various parts of the county. Radiation, Inc., was founded in 1950 by Homer Denius and George Shaw in old barracks at the Melbourne Airport. The company designed and manufactured antenna systems, semi-conductors, and power systems for various missiles.

A Titan booster missile launched the Gemini 8 spacecraft into space on March 16, 1966. The two crew members for this mission were Neil A. Armstrong and David R. Scott. In all, the Gemini program launched ten successful missions, sending 20 astronauts into orbit. Courtesy, NASA

At the Cape Canaveral Air Force Station on November 16, 1963, President John F. Kennedy met with astronauts Gordon Cooper (next to Kennedy) and Virgil I. "Gus" Grissom. On the extreme right is G. Merritt Preston, then-manager of manned spacecraft Florida operations. Courtesy, NASA

President John F. Kennedy met with Mercury astronaut Walter Schirra during his tour of Cape Canaveral in November of 1963. Courtesy, NASA

It soon became the second largest employer (after Cape Canaveral) in Brevard.

In early 1960 Radiation moved to a large, modern plant in Palm Bay, and in 1967 the founders sold the company to the Harris Corporation. With Dr. Joseph Boyd as the new president, Harris continued to grow, enticing young families to South Brevard. In 1978 Harris, which by then had 30,000 employees worldwide, moved its corporate headquarters to Melbourne from Cleveland, Ohio. Under the leadership of John T. Hartley, chief executive officer and president, it has become Florida's largest industrial employer.

Also new in the early 1960s was Brevard Junior College, originally housed in the old Cocoa High School building, with Bruce Wilson serving as the first president. In 1963 a large campus of two-story brick buildings was dedicated on Clearlake Road in Cocoa. Soon after a fine arts building with a large theater was added, where residents from all parts of the 70-mile county enjoyed plays, lectures, and the Brevard Symphony Orchestra. Today there are three branches of Brevard Community College, located in Titusville, Melbourne, and Palm Bay. The school has grown to 30,000 full- and part-time students.

In addition, several private schools opened during this period, among them the already mentioned Florida Institute of Technology; Central Catholic High School, Brevard's only private upper school; and two Episcopal schools, St. Mark's in Cocoa and Holy Trinity in Melbourne. Many parochial schools were started throughout Brevard County, the oldest being Our Lady of Lourdes in Melbourne. Shelton Bible College, established in Cape Canaveral by radio evangelist Dr. Carl McIntire of New Jersey, closed in 1972 after several fires damaged buildings and adverse publicity lowered enrollment. Shelton College reopened in the Gateway to the Stars/Freedom Center owned by McIntire (formerly the Cape Canaveral Hilton).

The new four-story Brevard Hospital opened in 1962 on Hickory Street, Melbourne, providing 180 beds. Patients were transferred from the crowded wards and halls of the tiny hospital on U.S. 1 to this modern facility.

Brevard's residents needed more than a regular hospital, however. Engineers felt the stress of launching missiles and rockets safely, and on time. Uprooted families moving to a new environment with double-session schools, overcrowded hospitals, and few outlets for entertainment were particularly anxious and depressed. A *Melbourne Times* journalist reported that "Brevard has one of the highest rates of mental health problems in the nation." A mental health center was organized with offices in Rockledge on Barton Boulevard, and later a branch was started in Melbourne, known today as "Circles of Care."

As Brevard's population reached 84,000 in 1964, many needs remained unmet, especially social problems that had been swept under the rug for generations. Set in the Deep South, Brevard had always practiced segregation. That year, black members of the space community made known their dissatisfaction.

As Dr. Martin Luther King, Jr., led marches throughout the South to protest segregation, Brevard had demonstrations of its own. There were sit-ins at the lunch counters of Woolworth's in various shopping centers. Blacks demanded front-door access to movie theaters rather than through dirty alleys. They also resented having to sit in the balcony while paying the same price for their tickets as whites.

In 1954 the United States Supreme Court mandated integration of all the nation's schools. But by the mid-1960s schools in Brevard County had failed to comply. By 1964 the Brevard County School Board could no longer resist the pressures. The shoddy schools in "colored" towns were closed and black children registered at the bright new elementary schools recently built for white space workers' families.

None of this went unnoticed by the Ku Klux Klan, which burned crosses in South Melbourne and West Cocoa. Many white parents protested integration by pulling their children out of public schools and organizing all-white Christian schools or teaching them at home.

Interracial advisory committees were set up in each town to ease the transition to integration. In May 1964 Melbourne City Commissioner Nathan Friedland met with local leaders to calm racial tensions. Melbourne blacks only asked for three changes: use of bathrooms in restaurants, better theater facilities, and access to the local golf courses.

A committee of 12 was appointed, with Mayor Grady White presiding. Some of the black leaders present included pioneer businessman John Brothers; U.F. Gibson, principal of then all-black Stone High School; and Henry Jackson, president of the local NAACP. As a result of these talks, one fourth of the restaurant owners agreed to a 60-day trial integration of their facilities. The Melbourne Country Club was desegregated.

Brevard schools were integrated in the fall of 1964. That year Eau Gallie High School opened with several black students in the sophomore class. The first blacks to graduate from EGHS did so in 1967.

That same year, Ted Nichols, a teacher at Stone High School, qualified for a seat on the Melbourne City Commission. There were 792 registered black voters on the books and Nichols, then 29, became the first black elected to public office in the county, winning a two-year term.

As most black children lived on the mainland, schools in the beach areas were integrated only after busing was implemented. Overall, desegregation throughout Brevard went smoothly, with few incidents.

Other changes came to the county as well. A major publishing event took

The imposing Apollo/Saturn 500-F, pictured here in 1966 at the Kennedy Space Center, was used as a test vehicle to verify launch facilities, train launch crews, and to develop test and checkout procedures. Courtesy, NASA

place on March 21, 1966, when Allen H. Neuharth, a Gannett executive, bought the *Cocoa Tribune* to create a new newspaper especially for the Space Coast. He called it *TODAY*. Neuharth drew top young journalists to his infant publication, used extensive color, and tossed free copies on every front lawn in Brevard for a month. The paper quickly captured the county's daily and Sunday circulation, although it continued to receive competition from the *Orlando Sentinel*. The offices and plant were in Cocoa.

Neuharth built a lavish oceanfront home in Cocoa Beach. From there he ran the immense Gannett Corporation upon becoming chairman of the board. In 1982 he launched a new national daily, *USA TODAY*, which already has the largest circulation of any paper in the nation.

TODAY celebrated its 20th anniversary with the opening of the impressive Gannett Plaza on U.S. 1 in Melbourne. The 200,000 square foot building contains the editorial offices of the paper, now renamed *Florida TODAY*, and its state-of-the-art offset press that also prints three Brevard weeklies. Copy for the local edition of *USA TODAY* arrives via satellite dish on the grounds and is published here as well.

The 1960s were also a time of consolidation. Three cities in North Brevard—Titusville, Indian River City, and Whispering Hills—were incorporated as Titusville. In 1969 Eau Gallie and Melbourne also merged. Five names were proposed for the new city, and Melbourne won. Old-timers nevertheless continue to refer to the charming harbor city as Eau Gallie. Efforts were made to merge Cocoa and Rockledge, but Rockledge resisted, preferring to maintain its own identity.

This was also the period when the Air Force's giant intercontinental ballistic missile, the Titan II, was tested and readied for the two-man Gemini program. There were 10 successful Gemini missions with 20 astronauts placed in orbit. Perhaps the most exciting launches were Gemini 6 and 7, the first manned capsules to rendezvous in space. The final Gemini-Titan II was launched from Cape Canaveral on November 11, 1966.

Meanwhile, several probes of the moon had been attempted. Ranger 7 was launched on July 28, 1964, traveling 250,000 miles from the Cape to the moon. It relayed back thousands of photographs of the lunar surface, providing necessary information for later Apollo landings.

Again, American success was upstaged when Soviet scientists landed Luna 1 on the moon in 1966. Just a few months later Surveyor 1 leaped from its pad on Cape Canaveral to bring back information about lunar soil. Brevard began to prepare for America's greatest project.

Early in the 1960s NASA began to acquire huge blocks of land on Merritt Island west of Cape Canaveral in preparation for the proposed moon landing. Five hundred people had to be moved from their homes on the 80,000-acre tract. Three recreation areas, including popular beaches, and three towns were eliminated.

North Brevard began to prosper. Titusville was located directly across the river from the site chosen for the 52-story Vertical Assembly Building. Inside the world's largest structure, the 360-foot-tall Saturn rockets would be assembled.

The powerful Saturn V was to launch a crew of three into space with the objective of landing a man on the moon. A new concept of how to move the giant rocket three and a half miles from the assembly building to the launchpad was developed. A massive crawler—the size of a football field and weighing 6 million pounds—would move at a snail's pace on a bed of rocks. It sounded crazy, but it worked!

The new NASA Causeway was built just south of Titusville to provide direct access to the Kennedy Space Center. Naturally, all of this construction required a huge number of technical employees. Titusville was the closest city to the vast Kennedy Space Center, and as a result it began to grow. In 1958 Titusville pioneer Jesse Parrish, Jr., donated the land for the town's 28-bed hospital, to be named for his father, Jess Parrish. In 1966 Parrish, president of the Nevins Fruit Company, banker, and land and market investor, donated a large sum to add a seven-story tower with 200 beds. Parrish was inducted into the Citrus Hall of Fame in March 1988.

Titusville's skyscraper courthouse was completed in 1967. At the same time, the city got the Sears Town and Miracle City malls, office buildings for NASA contractors, a new post office, Astronaut High School, and seven new elementary schools. A city pier, a bigger library, and two country clubs, Sherwood and Royal Oak, were also built. Before you could blink, Titusville had 42 churches and

three radio stations. Between 1960 and 1970 the population grew from 6,000 in a mostly agrarian community of citrus groves and cattle ranches to a city of 30,615, based on the aerospace and electronics industries. The scene in North Brevard was much like the Gold Rush days of the Old West. The town grew faster than amenities could keep pace.

Space-related employment in Brevard County grew from 2,000 in 1960 to 27,000 in 1966. Support industries, construction, and education provided 54,000 new jobs. With many areas of the United States suffering recession, thousands of families moved to Brevard to better their circumstances.

The grand opening of Titusville's first shopping center took place in 1958. Originally named "The Big Apple," it is now called Sand Point Village. Courtesy, Bob Hudson

Since the space programs provided an abundance of employment opportunities, the population of Brevard County rapidly increased. In the fall of 1971 these members of the Apollo 16 program were hard at work on the Lunar Rover Vehicle. Courtesy, NASA

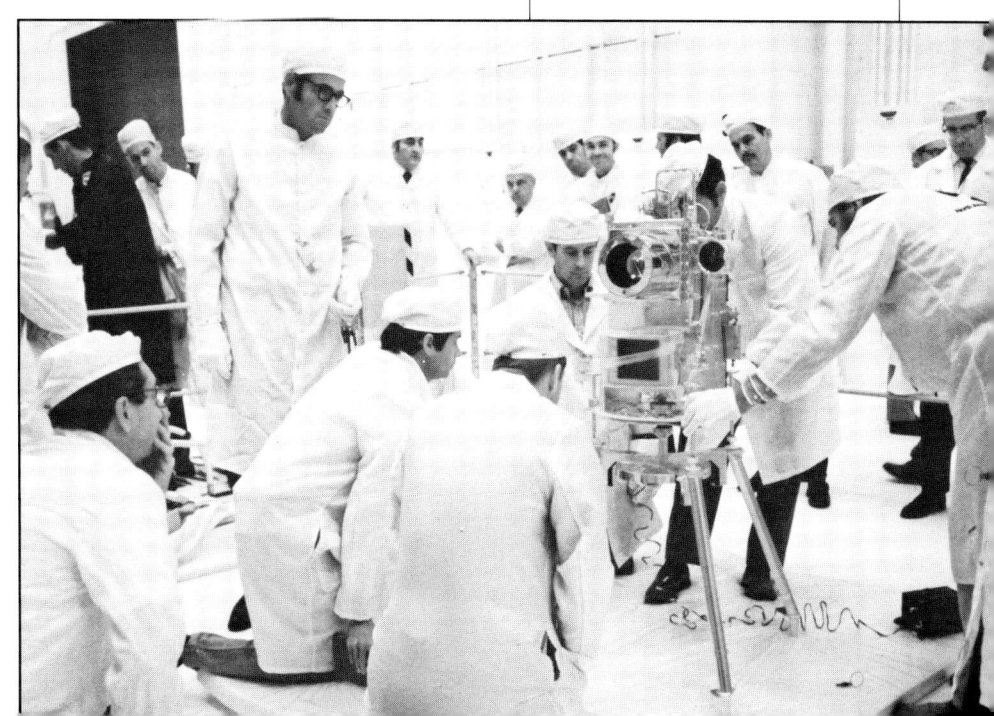

Vice President Hubert H. Humphrey attended the Hubert H. Humphrey Bridge dedication in Cocoa on March 1, 1968. Courtesy, Al and Bernice Stefurak

Brevard also capitalized on tourism. Long before Disney World existed, Titusville had the first family-oriented attraction: Johnny Weismuller's African Village. Years after it went defunct, escaped monkeys were seen scampering through the wilds of North Brevard. Another attraction was the replica of a Spanish galleon docked on the Indian River. For a small fee, tourists could go aboard and view gold and silver artifacts from Brevard's very own sunken treasure.

During the 1960s the whole county had treasure fever. Remains of the Spanish Plate Fleet, wrecked in a violent hurricane in 1715, were discovered off Sebastian Inlet. These galleons of the 11 vessel *flota* had been carrying millions in gold and silver back to Spain.

Using ancient maps and information from the Spanish archives, Kip Wagner of Sebastian was able to identify shadows under the sea as ballast stones of the sunken galleons. His discovery was worth millions, but how to exhume the treasure, and where to find the funds?

To finance the venture, Wagner approached several officers at Patrick Air Force Base, among them colonels Dan Thompson and Harry Cannon, and Captain John Jones. Together with experienced divers Del Long, Lou Ullian, Bob Johnson, Rex Stocker, Bob Marx, and Mel Fisher, they formed the Real Eight Company. Using suction pumps and tubes, they vacuumed away sand, uncovering biscuits of gold, thousands of gold doubloons, silver pieces of eight, jeweled crosses, rings, and chains.

The corporation first exhibited its finds in the lobby of a Satellite Beach bank. Later the owners built their own Museum of Sunken Treasure in the city of Cape Canaveral. Here they displayed cases of magnificent treasure, along with dioramas depicting the sunken ships and native divers retrieving what treasures they could. *National Geographic* did a story in its January 1965 issue, and documentaries and newscasts provided even more publicity. The octagonal-shaped museum was robbed and vandalized, closed, and has since been restored and used as a restaurant known as Diamond Lil's.

Several more causeways were built to relieve traffic congestion to and from the Cape during this period, including a toll road north of Cocoa called the Bennett

Causeway, and the Bee-Line Expressway to Orlando's airport. The county's first high-rise bridge connecting Cocoa to heavily populated Merritt Island was named for and dedicated by then-Vice President Hubert Humphrey. Through his efforts the Air Force and NASA picked up 80 percent of the cost. Later the Pineda Causeway north of Eau Gallie was built to provide quick evacuation of Patrick personnel and equipment in case of an attack or a major hurricane. Today Brevard has seven high-rise causeways spanning the Indian and Banana rivers.

With the giant Vertical Assembly Building completed and the first unmanned Apollo ready for launch, America was riding high on its space triumphs. Then followed one of the two saddest moments in the history of the space program. The first Apollo team of astronauts was burned to death during a routine flight readiness test of their launch vehicle.

Over the years, the county's residents had witnessed many missile failures; statistically, one in twenty was aborted. It was obvious that someday the same thing might happen to an astronaut. Yet a flash fire on the pad was not anticipated.

After the tragic deaths of Ed White, Virgil "Gus" Grissom, and Roger Chaffee, the Apollo program came to a halt. A spark had ignited the pure oxygen in the astronauts' cabin, and the entire space capsule had to be redesigned with additional safety considerations. "Fire is something we will never underestimate again," stated Dr. Kurt Debus, then director of NASA's Kennedy Space Center.

The installation of a safer escape system, the use of non-flammable space suits and an oxygen/nitrogen mix rather than pure oxygen in the capsule, and 1,500 other changes were made before the next Apollo mission took place. The delay resulted in the layoff of many highly trained members of the launch team. Large numbers of support personnel working for NASA contractors also were dismissed. Brevard's air of pride and excitement changed to one of mourning.

Although nine months passed before another Apollo launch was attempted, there were many other projects under way at the Cape, including weather and communication satellites, intercontinental ballistic missiles, and tests of the giant Saturn V engines. None of these were affected by layoffs resulting from the Apollo fire.

By 1968, after several unmanned test flights, all was ready for the first manned Apollo launch, designated Apollo 7. The brave astronauts aboard this monster rocket were Wally Schirra, Don Eisele, and Walter Cunningham, all veterans of the Gemini program. They sent back the first telecasts of our planet from space. Once again, America felt proud of the space program, as the astronauts orbited the earth for 11 days and splashed down safely.

First to leave earth's atmosphere and journey to the moon's were Apollo astronauts Frank Borman, James Lovell, and Bill Anders. Millions of hearts were touched as Borman read a passage from scripture while orbiting a full moon on Christmas Eve, 1968.

With each succeeding Apollo mission, Brevard was inundated by immense crowds, eager to view the dramatic

Three days before they perished in their Apollo capsule in a fire, Apollo astronauts (bottom to top) Virgil "Gus" Grissom, Edward White, and Roger Chaffee pose in front of the Apollo simulator on January 25, 1967. Courtesy, NASA

On May 20, 1969, the crew of Apollo 11 posed in front of the launch vehicle which would carry them to the moon. From left to right are: Neil A. Armstrong, Michael Collins, and Edwin E. Aldrin. Courtesy, NASA

launches. Many more tourists arrived for Apollos 9 and 10, but even their numbers paled in comparison to the scene on July 16, 1969, as Apollo 11 prepared to lift off for the first manned landing on the moon.

A million people jammed the roads and causeways around Merritt Island, Titusville, and Cocoa Beach, filling every possible viewing site on beaches, jettys, and parks. Trapped in hopeless traffic jams, most just stepped out of their cars where they were stopped to watch the historic event.

For days prior to July 16, commercial jets and private planes buzzed overhead transporting VIPs, journalists from every nation, and newscasters. President Johnson, Ethiopian Emperor Haile Selassie, the King and Queen of Belgium, and the heads of many nations, diplomats, generals, movie stars, and millionaires—together totaling 20,000 people—filled the VIP viewing stands beside the Vertical Assembly Building. Across the way thousands of journalists from all over the world filled every seat in the giant press booth. Mary Bubb of Reuters, who always attracted attention with her giant hats embodying the theme of each mission, sported an eagle, the insignia of Apollo 11. In temporary trailers and studios behind the stands, Walter Cronkite, Jules Bergman, and Roy Neal waited to tell the world the news. Photographers set up their expensive equipment around the field in front of the packed press stand.

Every motel in Brevard and as far away as Orlando was filled to capacity. Children waved flags and held up banners. The air was filled with excitement and goodwill, resembling a giant carnival rather than a life-or-death scientific achievement.

At 8:32 a.m. on that historic day, all eyes were directed toward Pad 39A, where Apollo astronauts Neil Armstrong, Michael Collins, and "Buzz" Aldrin waited to be hurled into space on a tail of fire. As NASA's Jack King announced the words, "All systems go," prayers were lifted, hearts beat faster. Then came the final countdown, "Three, two, one." Giant flames shot out from under the Saturn V's engines. Slowly at first, the 363-foot rocket lifted off its pad. Faster and faster, ever higher, it flashed in the morning sunlight. "We have lift-off," shouted King. Powerful aftershocks rattled the metal roof of the press stand, as newsmen, VIPs, and ordinary folks cheered and applauded. Many wept.

Journalists rushed down the steps of the stand to get a view of the first stage separation. At last the spaceship *Columbia*, by then just a tiny dot, disappeared from sight. The rocket's contrail finally disintegrated into thin wisps of cotton. It was over. Then followed the biggest traffic jam in history, as millions of viewers waited bumper-to-bumper to get off the Cape or out of the vicinity of the Cape where they had witnessed the incredible event.

On July 20, most of the world came to a standstill to watch the dramatic moment on television as Neil Armstrong carefully set the Lunar Lander down on the surface of the moon, and announced, "The Eagle has landed!" Still more exhilarating was the sight of Armstrong in his bulky suit descending the steps from the spaceship and taking that "one giant leap for mankind."

Engineers at their consoles in Mission Control, Houston, cheered and clapped and passed out cigars. It was 1969. Brevard's thousands of engineers and tech-

On July 20, 1969, during the Apollo 11 mission, Edwin E. Aldrin, Jr., prepares to take his first step onto the moon's surface. This moment was photographed by Neil A. Armstong, who had already achieved the distinction of being the first man on the moon. Courtesy, NASA

Astronaut Edwin E. Aldrin, Jr., was the second man to walk on the surface of the moon during the historic Apollo 11 mission in 1969. Courtesy, NASA

nicians had fulfilled President Kennedy's dream of landing an American on the moon before the end of the decade.

At the same time, the black community organized a journey of another kind, a Poor People's March to protest poverty and the failure of Congress to address their needs. Led by national and state NAACP leaders and local black clergy, a procession of mule-drawn carts and thousands of people marched from Cocoa to the entrance of the Kennedy Space Center, where they camped out. With thousands of newsmen in the area for Apollo 11, they received a great deal of publicity.

Apollo 17, the first nighttime lift-off, was also the last lunar landing mission, signaling the end of the Apollo program. This final launch was sent into space from the Kennedy Space Center at 12:33 a.m. (EST) on December 7, 1972, and was manned by Eugene A. Cernan, Ronald E. Evans, and Harrison H. Schmitt. Courtesy, NASA

TRAGEDY & TRIUMPH

Apollo 17, the final Apollo mission to the moon, splashed down in 1972. During the epic years of the Apollo program, American astronauts spent 900 hours exploring the moon's surface and conducting scientific experiments. The phenomenal growth of Brevard County now came to a grinding halt. No further research or testing was required for subsequent Apollo missions. Thousands of highly specialized technicians were laid off. With each succeeding payday, pink slips were distributed—totaling 12,000 between 1970 and 1972. By 1975 Brevard's unemployment rate soared to 12 percent.

The Skylab Program, an extension of the Mercury-Gemini-Apollo space programs, began in the spring of 1973. Skylab was designed to expand our knowledge of manned earth-orbital operations and to carry out selected scientific, technological, and medical investigations. This artist's rendering depicts the space station in orbit over the Atlantic Ocean. Courtesy, NASA

For people accustomed to high pay and plush living, the shock of such a dramatic shift in lifestyle brought on mental and family problems. A pall of fear and uncertainty hung over every community from Palm Bay to Titusville, replacing the pride and excitement of the 1960s. In many developments, "For Sale" signs stood in every yard.

Support services went out of business and construction came to a halt, creating a severe recession. Large building projects were abandoned, and apartment and shopping complexes stood empty and unfinished. Bankruptcy claims escalated. There were long lines at the Florida state employment offices, but no work was available.

Next followed an exodus of high-tech scientists and engineers. Many moved to California's Silicon Valley or electronic manufacturing areas like Dallas or Boston. Others trained for new careers that offered more stability than the Cape's roller coaster economy. Many older engineers and scientists took early retirement.

It was a bad time for all residents of Brevard. It would be eight long years before the Space Shuttle would generate a return to prosperity. It was at this time that pressure was exerted to restore the Cape's historic name, and in 1973 it was renamed Cape Canaveral by Congress.

During those depressing times there was one ray of hope: Walt Disney was planning an immense attraction in central Florida, one hour away from Brevard's wide, white beaches. Disney officials secretively began buying sections of oceanfront in South Melbourne Beach. Brevard was going to ride on Disney's coattails, or so everyone surmised. Although the proposed beach attraction never materialized, Brevard profited in many ways from proximity to the Magic Kingdom. Better roads were built connecting Melbourne to Kissimmee and Cocoa to Orlando. Tourists visiting Disney World spent a few extra days of their vacations at the beach. In 1982, after State Road 192 was widened to four lanes, fast-food restaurants and malls mushroomed along it. Oceanfront hotels in Cocoa

Beach and Indialantic sprang from the sand as if by magic.

Despite funding cuts and a reduced work force, the Kennedy Space Center and Cape Canaveral Air Force Station initiated several new projects. One such mission was Skylab, a prototype space station capable of supporting three astronauts for months. From their maneuverable spacecraft the crew would make scientific investigations, test new equipment, and report on global weather conditions.

Skylab 2 left the Kennedy Space Center launchpad on May 25, 1973, with Alan Bean, Jack Lousma, and Owen Garriott aboard. They remained in orbit for 28 days. Other Skylab missions followed on July 28 and November 28 of that year. Pioneer 10, launched March 2, 1972, became the first man-made object to leave our solar system, crossing the orbit of Neptune in 1982.

Nearby, on Merritt Island, a three-mile landing strip was under construction for the future Space Shuttle, *Columbia*, scheduled for launch in 1978. Unlike previous expendable space vehicles, this seven-passenger orbiter could land like an airplane and be used again and again. Alternate landing fields were laid out in the Mojave desert at Edwards Air Force Base and at White Sands, New Mexico.

The cold war eased a bit when the United States and the Soviet Union joined hands in the 1975 Apollo/Soyuz project. On July 15, Russia launched two cosmonauts from a site at Kazakhstan, while America launched "Deke" Slayton, Vance Brand, and Thomas Stafford from Kennedy Space Center. The two spacecraft docked July 17, and the teams conducted joint experiments and ate together high above the troubled earth. It

The three prime crews of the Skylab Program, shown in this illustration, were selected on the basis of astronautical, scientific, and medical skills. Each of the three mission crews consisted of a commander, science pilot, and pilot, with the First Skylab Mission crew designated as Charles Conrad, Jr., Joseph P. Kerwin, and Paul J. Weitz. Courtesy, NASA

This elderly woman relaxes on the porch of the Brevard Hotel, where she has lived for the past 26 years. Since the late 1960s the average age in Brevard County has risen sharply. Photo by Ron Lindsey

Facing page: The successful launch of the first Space Shuttle, Columbia, in 1981 promised a new season of prosperity and growth for Brevard County. Courtesy, NASA

was a significant step toward better international relations.

But Brevard, like much of the nation, had its share of social problems in the 1970s. As drug abuse worsened, many dedicated people worked to help Brevard's troubled young people. "His House" was a Christian drug rehabilitation center on East New Haven Avenue. The antiquated house, built in 1907, is now Nannie Lee's Strawberry Mansion, a top-ranked dining facility. Another rehabilitation center was downtown Cocoa's Renaissance House, which since has been razed for additional parking space. Christ Is the Answer Rescue Mission (CITA) in South Melbourne is housed in a former hotel. Founded by Johnny Ellison in 1969, CITA now offers shelter to homeless men and abused women. Merritt Island's "Crosswinds" today cares for 400 runaway and abused teenagers a year.

In the 1970s a new element, the retiree, appeared. Homes left vacant by departing technical workers were acquired simply by taking over monthly payments. Brevard demographics changed greatly, the average age rising from 25 in 1969 to 35 in the 1980s. As more older couples replaced young families, more medical facilities were required. Brevard Hospital expanded to 331 beds in 1971, and was quickly surrounded by doctors' offices, laboratories, and nursing homes. That same year, Cape Canaveral Hospital in Cocoa Beach added a four-story wing.

Wuesthoff Hospital in Rockledge had a $30-million, 300,000 square foot expansion, including the county's first hospice and a fitness center. It soon became Central Brevard's primary employer, with 1,200 medical specialists and support personnel.

The Reverend Alex Boyer, then rector of Holy Trinity Episcopal Church, secured federal funds to erect two 12-story buildings in the heart of Melbourne. Providing affordable housing for older residents, Trinity Towers East was completed in 1969 and Trinity Towers West opened in 1971. Trinity Towers South, which provides both food and lodging, opened in 1982 on New Haven Avenue. Meals on Wheels, adult day care, and senior citizen clubs, as well as free noontime dinners, are also available.

During the 1970s, environmental considerations also became more important to many, as thousands of untouched wooded acres were taken over by apartments, malls, office buildings, and parking lots. In addition, the Indian River was being polluted by sewage, manufacturing effluents, and ever-increasing boat traffic. Brevard residents took action.

Several groups were organized, such as the Turtle Coast Sierra Club, Save the Manatee, and Sea Turtle Preservation Society. Not long after, the Department of the Interior set aside 120,000 acres for the Canaveral National Seashore. Local naturalists dedicated the Erna Nixon Hammock and Park, Palm Bay's Turkey Creek Sanctuary, and Cocoa's Johnny Johnson Nature Center at the Brevard Museum of History and Natural Science. Visitors to the Merritt Island Wildlife Refuge and Bird Sanctuary counted 310 species of birds in 1987 during the annual Christmas bird count at the Indian River Audubon Society. However, over the last few years the annual bird count has dropped alarmingly. Several species are now on the endangered list, among them the Florida scrub jay and the brown pelican. The seaside dusky sparrow is already extinct.

Despite ecological concerns, Brevard continued to grow. In the 1960s several sections of Melbourne's four-lane U.S. 1 were rerouted to less populated divisions. When Melbourne and Eau Gallie merged in 1969, the roadway was renamed Harbor City Boulevard. Roads continued to cut through new areas, such as South Patrick Drive, while old ones were improved and widened. Unfortunately, this upgrading required removing the tall Australian pines that had arched over A1A in Indialantic and Cocoa Beach since the 1920s.

By the late 1970s Brevard's economy had stabilized. No longer totally dependent on the Space Center, it had diversified to include high-tech manufacturing and services such as medical care, shopping centers, entertainment, and tourism.

"Gus" Hipp, the beloved late city manager of Rockledge, transformed former citrus groves into an industrial park. He enticed corporations to move to Central Brevard, bringing the Norsk-Hydro Aluminum Works of Norway to town. Rockledge remained primarily a bedroom community, as more and more groves were bought by developers to construct tract houses.

As the hour approached for the launch of America's first Space Shuttle, engineers transferred to the Space Coast once again and the local economy picked up. On April 12, 1981, the 120-foot spaceship *Columbia* rose from Pad 39 at the Kennedy Space Center. Propelled by two solid rocket boosters, it quickly disappeared into the morning sky. More than a million people swarmed into North Brevard and the Cocoa Beach area to view the spectacular event. Prosperity once again blessed the county.

This time North Brevard profited most. The Space Shuttle program employed over 14,000 people, many of whom chose to settle in the sparsely populated area around Titusville. Another boom, much like the one in the 1960s, enlivened the area. A new community, Port St. John, was begun by the General Development Corporation in South Titusville. Providing inexpensive housing, it has grown to a population of 7,000!

Merritt Island, a vast area between the Banana and Indian rivers east of Cocoa, has never been incorporated. This did not prevent tremendous growth north and south of the 520 Causeway. Brevard's first giant shopping center, Merritt Square Mall, opened in 1969 with 85 chain and independent stores. It also contained the first mini-theaters, offering a

choice of six feature films. Automobile dealerships and restaurants line both sides of State Road 520.

Port Canaveral was again enlarged and deepened for Navy tracking ships, nuclear submarines, and cruise ships. With three home-ported cruise ships and 12 ports-of-call by other vessels, Port Canaveral hosted 728,886 passengers in 1987. This made the port the third largest volume cruise passenger port in the United States. Such luxury liners as the *Queen Elizabeth II*, *Europa*, and *Astor* have called at Port Canaveral, providing passengers a chance to visit Kennedy Space Center, area beaches, and central Florida's famous attractions.

Commercial tours of the Kennedy Space Center began in 1963. From a small facility on U.S. 1 south of Titusville, the Space Center expanded onto Merritt Island in 1966, adding a large visit-

Facing page, top: Astronauts John Young and Robert Crippen take a moment to speak with reporters after the triumphant landing of the first Space Shuttle flight in 1981. Courtesy, NASA

Facing page, bottom: Port Canaveral, first established in the late 1870s, was later dredged and enlarged in the 1950s and today accommodates several cruise lines as well as other large military and commercial seagoing vessels. Photo by Ed Malles

Left: Spaceport USA at the Kennedy Space Center has provided tours to the public since the early 1960s. The Rocket Garden, pictured here, is a favorite attraction for all visitors. Courtesy, TW Recreational Services, Spaceport USA

Children and adults alike delight in the many exhibits and shops to be seen at Spaceport USA. Courtesy, TW Recreational Services, Spaceport USA

ors' center featuring exhibits of Mercury capsules, moon rovers, space suits, and souvenir shops. In 1980 the I-MAX Theater was added, projecting movies about the Space Shuttle on a five-story screen. Spaceport USA, managed and operated by TW Recreational Services, welcomed 2.5 million visitors in 1987. Today, visitors may tour the Kennedy Space Center and the Air Force Museum on Cape Canaveral. Brevard also has a planetarium located on the Cocoa campus of Brevard Community College, offering the documentary "The Space Shuttle: An American Adventure" and many other shows.

An escalation in interest rates during the Carter administration brought most construction to a halt. This was a difficult period for builders, realtors, and home buyers, who were priced out of the market. Following the steady reduction in interest rates during the Reagan administration, a welcome upturn in business and construction has continued throughout the 1980s. Once a scarcity, rental apartments have been overbuilt, so that many complexes offer incentives like gifts or a month's free rent to maintain full occupancy.

Not every retiree could afford an oceanfront condo, or even a landlocked town house, so many moved into mobile home parks. Today's parks offer clubhouses, heated swimming pools, and luxurious double-wide manufactured homes. A few of these parks have grown to mammoth size, larger than many Brevard towns. Barefoot Bay, near Sebastian on U.S. 1, is a complete community in itself, with its own post office, golf course, 776-foot fishing pier, beachside access, and nearby medical facilities. Over 6,313 people now live there in 3,714 homes. Similar mobile home communities are Lantern Village in West Melbourne; Island Lakes, Merritt Island; Holiday Haven, stretching from the river to the ocean in Melbourne Beach; and Pinewood Mobile Village in Scottsmoor, Brevard's northernmost city.

Also popular are airstream yachts. Over 1,000 winter each year in the 28-acre Port-O-Call at Melbourne Airport, adding $2 million to South Brevard's economy, according to George Pittman, deputy director of the airport.

Brevard's first hospital was renamed Holmes Regional Medical Center in 1977 in honor of the late James E. Holmes, chairman of the hospital board for many years. In 1983 a $43-million, eight-story tower was opened, containing an additional 288 beds. Today, Holmes Regional offers a total of 528 beds, with a staff of 135 specialists and 1,300 employees. A three-story parking garage was recently completed.

During the 1970s and 1980s Brevard's arts and culture attracted greater interest and blossomed. In January 1978 the Brevard Museum of History and Natural Science opened on Michigan Avenue in Cocoa. The 6,000 square foot building houses Indian and pioneer exhibits and fossils of creatures that once made Brevard their home. But there was no art museum, other than traveling collections from the Ringling Museum in Sarasota. A committee spearheaded by Lucy Gunthrope raised funds for the Brevard Art Center and Museum (BACAM), which opened in 1978 on Highland Avenue in old Eau Gallie. Marcia Denius served as the first president.

Using the $100,000 gift of Elizabeth Winchester, the Brevard Symphony purchased the two-story Victorian building next door in 1984. This became "Symphony House," headquarters for the orchestra's office personnel. The symphony now operates on an annual budget of $300,000, under the direction of its new permanent artistic director, Kypros Markou.

With the active support of the 750 members of the Brevard Arts Council, exhibitions and competitions such as the Indialantic Seaside, Cocoa Village, Cocoa Beach, and Downtown Melbourne art shows followed one after the other. Brevard's first all-professional symphony, the Florida Space Coast Philharmonic, made its debut on July 4, 1986, under the baton of Maestro Maria Tunicka. The Brevard Symphony's youth orchestra, conducted by Willem Bertsch, was started in 1985. And in April 1988 the $12.5-million, 2,000-seat Center for the Performing Arts on the Melbourne campus of Brevard Community College opened with the musical "Singin' in the Rain." Another new organization in South Brevard is the all-professional Ensemble Theatre in Le Gallerie Arcade. It has brought such famed actors as Jose Ferrer and Noel Harrison to the area.

Highland Avenue, formerly run-down and dingy, was spruced up with new curbs and landscaping to become the home of art galleries and antique shops. Meanwhile, the Melbourne Police Department outgrew its Highland facility and moved to new quarters on NASA Boulevard. In 1984 BACAM purchased the former police station, and with volunteer workers transformed it into one of the finest small museums in the country.

The South Brevard Junior League felt that children and science were being bypassed. With the aid of a committee led by Jennifer Marx, they created the Space Coast Science Center. Dr. Peter Zies served as its first president. The new organization moved into the former quarters of the art museum, setting up hands-on exhibits geared toward children. All three organizations—the Space Coast Science Center, BACAM, and the Brevard Symphony Orchestra—unite in April for a fundraiser called the "Highland Fling."

The South Brevard Historical Society is one of the area's oldest organizations, for many years operating a museum in the old Henegar School. The society was required to move out when the building was restored to become headquarters for the Brevard Regional Arts Group (BRAG), and is now readying the original 1926 Melbourne High School, located next door, to house its extensive collection. Brevard also has two other small collections, the McLarty Museum of Sunken Treasure south of Sebastian Inlet, and the recently opened "House of 1916" in Grant.

Four major festivals draw visitors from all over the country. The oldest is the Grant Seafood Festival, held each February since 1966. In the winter of 1987 the small community served dinners to 50,000 people! The Port Canaveral Seafood Festival, sponsored by the Cocoa Beach Area Chamber of Commerce, the Canaveral Port Authority, and the local seafood industry, takes place in March. During its fifth season, it topped Grant's, with 60,000 attending. Two Oktoberfests are held in the county—one in Titusville, the other in Melbourne. Both feature Bavarian food, music, and costumes.

Brevard is also host to major athletic events. The International Sailing Races are held annually on the Indian River. Since 1984 the 20-member Olympic Board Sailing Team has practiced north of the Eau Gallie Causeway. The Panthers, Florida Institute of Technology's rowing team, can be seen sculling on the Banana River off Indian Harbour Beach. F.I.T. has won many national and international trophies, outracing Yale and Princeton!

The Suntree Classic and the Senior PGA golf tournaments are held at the Suntree Country Club, drawing players of the caliber of Jack Nicklaus. In addition, the annual Labor Day Surfing Contest, sponsored by the National Kidney Foundation, generates excitement. Ron Jons, the world famous surf shop in Cocoa Beach, also co-sponsors a surfing tournament each Easter weekend at Canaveral Pier.

Another exciting event is the Valiant Air Command Show at Spaceport Executive Airport in Titusville. World War II planes engage in dogfights and aerobatics, with the fabled Flying Tigers participating. For the past 100 years, sport fishing in the Atlantic Ocean and Indian and St. Johns rivers has lured thousands to

Surfing is one of the numerous water sports to be enjoyed along the coast of Brevard County. Photo by Ed Malles

An airboat ride through Brevard's waterways is a favorite activity that combines sightseeing with the thrill of speed. Photo by Ed Malles

In 1960 hurricane Donna swept through Brevard County leaving destruction in its wake. The Titusville High School, pictured here, was seriously damaged. Courtesy, Bob Hudson

Brevard County. Port Canaveral is the site of the world's largest offshore sport fishing tournament.

Florida is the spring training location for many professional baseball teams, and for many years the Houston Astros made Cocoa their winter home, playing at the stadium off I-95 and 520. The Minnesota Twins still come to Melbourne for their spring practice.

Brevard County is also home to a large number of writers, many of them members of the Kennedy Space Center Press Corps. The Canaveral Press Club has entertained astronauts and anchormen, and prides itself on a fabulous annual Page One Ball. About 130 authors —including Nobel nominee Patrick Smith— belong to the Florida Space Coast Writer's Conference. Similar organizations are the Cape Canaveral Branch of the National League of American Penwomen, The Scribblers, and the Space Coast Playwrights Workshop.

Brevard County has been struck by several devastating hurricanes in the past, including Donna in 1960 and David in 1979. A severe drought in 1982 lowered Lake Washington, South Brevard's water source, to dangerous levels, but 1984 brought more water than anyone bargained for when local beaches received a terrible beating from the "No Name" storm on Thanksgiving weekend. Cocoa Beach's Pelican Landing Resort almost fell into the sea, and total damage topped $10 million, with $4.7 million of it at Patrick Air Force Base.

Undeterred by disaster, Brevard's economic growth continued. South Brevard finally got its own major shopping center in 1982, when the Edward J. DeBartolo Corporation developed Melbourne Square Mall on former pastureland at Evans Road and 192. The 1.2 million square foot mall houses five major department stores, including Ivey's and Burdines, 130 smaller stores, and 15 restaurants. Indialantic suffered a setback when several of its long-established fashion shops on Fifth Avenue moved to "The Oaks," a block south of the new mall.

The first high-rise bridge in South Brevard was the Pineda Causeway, built to provide access to Patrick Air Force Base and as an escape route in case of natural disaster. A $12-million high-rise bridge was begun in 1980 to replace the old Kouwen-Hoven drawbridge to Indialantic. Both lanes were finally completed in

Astronaut Sally Ride arrives at the Shuttle Landing Facility at the Kennedy Space Center on June 15, 1983, prior to her historic mission on the Space Shuttle Challenger. *Courtesy, NASA*

April 1985. The replacement of the old Eau Gallie bridge was all that remained to make beach area travel and yachting perfect. Construction began in the mid-1980s and was completed in 1988.

Melbourne's regional airport continues to serve both Brevard and Indian River counties as a stop for major carriers. The facility reported an increase in traffic from 256,211 passengers in 1972 to 495,622 in 1988. Since 1973 federal grants totaling $10.7 million have made possible the lengthening of landing strips for larger jets. In June 1988 ground was broken for an expanded terminal. Several new airlines are expected to serve the enlarged airport.

No longer dependent on space-related industries, Brevard residents nonetheless were still interested in everything at the Kennedy Space Center. Sally Ride, America's first woman in space, as well as Guion Bluford, the first black astronaut, made history as they lifted off aboard the successful Space Shuttle *Challenger*. Brevardians keenly watched the launch on January 12, 1986, because their own U.S. Congressman, Bill Nelson, was a member of the crew. After each landing the Shuttle was returned to Kennedy Space Center "piggyback" on a modified Boeing 747, to be refurbished in the giant Vertical Assembly Building and rolled out again for the next launch.

Thus it was on January 28, 1986, that schoolchildren were recessed to watch the *Challenger* carry America's first teacher/astronaut into space. Retirees and housewives lined beaches in the chilly morning hours, and office workers stayed glued to portable radios. Having followed 24 successful Shuttle missions, an accident could not have been further from their minds as the countdown approached.

Veteran rocket watchers were hardly surprised when a "hold" was called due to the unusually cold weather. Ice had formed in many areas of the county, even on the Space Shuttle itself. Anticipating a cancellation, most Brevard residents went about their business. Then over radios and television came the unexpected announcement—the countdown had resumed.

At 11:38 a.m. thousands of children, residents, and tourists waited outdoors to catch a glimpse of the huge rocket blasting into the clear blue sky. What they saw was a chilling and confusing sight. In-

The ill-fated Challenger *launched at 11:38 a.m. on January 28, 1986, from the Kennedy Space Center as thousands of spectators, only seconds later, watched in horror as the* Challenger *exploded, killing all seven crew members. Photo, courtesy, NASA*

stead of one wide contrail, there were numerous fragmented wisps, and bright objects appeared to be falling from the sky; the *Challenger* had exploded and the two women and five men aboard had been killed instantly before the eyes of millions of stunned viewers.

The Shuttle missions had become so routine to Brevard residents that crowds had diminished with each launch, except for this special one that carried the young teacher, Christa McAuliffe. Other members of the crew who died in the explosion were Judy Resnik, Gregory B. Jarvis, Francis Scobee, Michael J. Smith, Robert McNair, and Ellison Onizuka. Saddest of all was the picture of McAuliffe's small children waiting at the VIP site to see their mother ride off into space. Instead they witnessed her death.

The subsequent investigation focused on several questions: Why had the *Challenger* been launched on a freezing cold morning? Why had the faulty O-rings responsible for the accident been approved?

Once again NASA suffered a lengthy setback. The O-rings, sealing segments of the solid rocket booster, had to be redesigned before the next Space Shuttle could go to the pad. As in 1966 and 1969 there were cutbacks at the Kennedy Space Center.

By the mid-1980s, however, Brevard's economy had diversified sufficiently to forestall the usual resulting recession. But with the *Challenger*'s explosion, America's supremacy in space appeared as lost as the Shuttle. Project after project was put on hold, both at Cape Canaveral Air Force Station and the Kennedy Space Center. Launches were scrubbed, failed, blew apart, or never reached their destination. Brevard's contribution to the space effort became more and more disappointing.

The victims of the *Challenger* were not forgotten. Funds were raised for a memorial on the grounds of the Florida Institute of Technology, and a major million-dollar memorial is planned for the Kennedy Space Center. The latter, to be housed at NASA's Spaceport USA, will honor all astronauts who have died in the service of their country.

Despite the space industry's troubles, Brevard's businesses, banks, schools, arts, and sports continued to flourish in the late 1980s. Several giant oceanfront hotels were completed: the Hiltons of Melbourne, Melbourne Beach, and Cocoa Beach; the Ramada Inn in Satellite Beach; the Howard Johnson Plaza in Cocoa Beach; and the Radisson and Quality Court in Indialantic. Soon after Melbourne's Airport Hilton opened at Rialto Place, the posh and private Coast Club made its debut on the top floor of the Rialto's Sun Bank building. Not long after, Titusville got its own private club, the elegant, Spanish-style La Cita.

Palm Bay, incorporated in 1960 and once one of Brevard's smallest communities, is today the fastest growing and the second largest Brevard community after Melbourne. The city's population is 50,000, and its 63 square mile area make it Florida's fifth largest community. In 1987 its chamber of commerce merged with Melbourne's, and is now called the Greater South Brevard Area Chamber of Commerce. General Development's Palm Bay community of Port Malabar has 200 housing starts per month.

The same period which saw construction of shopping plazas and banks on almost every corner in Brevard also brought concern that our natural treasures and our past were disappearing under concrete and macadam. Naturalists did not allow this to pass unnoticed. A much-needed dredging of Sebastian Inlet was delayed while 60 resident terns completed their mating. Signs are posted in canals and waterways warning boaters to "slow for manatees." Only 1,200 of these gentle creatures still exist in Florida waters.

Similarly, funds were raised to restore aging churches, public buildings, and riverfront Victorian homes. Paperwork was rushed through to list antiquated buildings on the National Register of Historic Places. To date, five have made it: Melbourne's 1926 Ice Plant; the 625-foot Melbourne Beach Pier, originally built in 1889 and restored in 1985; St. Gabriel's Episcopal Church in Titusville, built in 1888; Cocoa's 1916 Porcher House; and Palm Bay's St. Joseph's Catholic Church, built in 1914. Three more of Titusville's 200 historic buildings have recently been nominated to the register.

To celebrate America's Bicentennial on July 4, 1976, Melbourne's Bicentennial Commission published a history of the city. Throughout Brevard there were parades with participants in colonial costumes, yacht races, band concerts, picnics, and fireworks over the Indian River. "Honor America" collected enough money to purchase and house a replica of the Liberty Bell. Its Memorial Museum in Wells Park, Melbourne, offers visual aids and exhibits about our country's history.

The late 1980s also saw many centennial celebrations. Rockledge and Titusville both reached 100th birthdays in 1987, while Melbourne celebrated its centennial in 1988. Holy Trinity in Melbourne celebrated its centenary in 1985; St. Gabriel's in Titusville celebrated its 100th anniversary in January 1988; Cocoa Beach had its 60th anniversary on May 22, 1985; and Cocoa celebrated its centennial in March 1988, with an outdoor drama, "Pioneers of the River-Ridge," written for the event by Ada Coats Williams, who married the great-great-grandson of Rockledge's co-founder, Hiram Smith Williams.

Many of these milestones were recorded in published histories, and most were occasions to dress up in pioneer and Victorian costumes, wave the flag, march in parades, and organize tours of restored areas.

Citrus, once the county's main export, continues to be important to North Brevard's economy. Local groves and plants produced 3.2 million boxes of fruit, adding $9 million in income last year.

Titusville, the county seat, experienced several changes. The overcrowded jail was closed and inmates moved to a new facility in Sharpes. Following charges that employees were being exposed to cancer-causing asbestos in the 1967 courthouse, the building underwent treatment at a cost of several million dollars. Meanwhile, files, trials, and personnel were transferred to temporary quarters around town. No decision has been reached about the construction or location of a new courthouse.

New, specialized hospitals opened during this period; the Sea Pines Rehabilitation Hospital and the Devereux Children's Hospital both serve the greater Melbourne area. A 60-bed drug and alcohol dependency treatment center for adolescents, the Community Psychiatric Hospital, operates in Palm Bay. Satellite clinics for Wuesthoff and Cape Canaveral hospitals have sprung up all over Central Brevard.

Packed with tourists seeking recreation in the Florida sunshine, the Holiday Inn at Melbourne Beach is a fine example of the large oceanside hotels built in the 1980s. Photo by Tony Arruza/Southern Stock Photos

The Ramada Inn near Satellite Beach is one of many new hotels springing up in Brevard County. Photo by Ron Lindsey

Through its tragedy and triumph the Space Shuttle program and the continuing exploration of the mysteries of space assure Brevard County growth and vitality for years to come. Courtesy, NASA

No longer a one-industry county, Brevard today is an economically diverse area, with high-tech manufacturing the major industry. There are 10 Fortune 500 corporations represented here, including such big names as Titusville's McDonnell Douglas, Lockheed, Grumman, Hughes, and Edwards Aircraft. Cocoa Beach and the city of Cape Canaveral have ITT, EG&G, RCA, Boeing, Bendix, and Pan American World Services. In addition to the Harris Corporation, the large plants of Documation, Rockwell-Collins, Dictaphone, DBA Systems, and Regency Electronics are located in South Brevard.

Families and retirees continue to come to Brevard County to enjoy its unparalleled quality of life. The area offers affordable housing, high pay, a low crime rate, and an unemployment rate of only 4.3 percent. Uncle Sam also brings big bucks to Brevard. U.S. military forces poured $1.6 billion into Brevard in 1987. This work force of 13,932 is spread out over the Eastern Space and Missile Center, Patrick Air Force Base, Cape Canaveral Air Force Station, Navy submarines and jets, and Coast Guard ships and helicopters. Payments to local physicians from military families, for example, totaled over $9.2 million in a recent year, in spite of the presence of the Patrick Air Force Base Hospital. Roughly 14,000 retired military personnel live in the vicinity of the base itself, with an additional 40,000 from adjacent counties using the facilities.

With a present population of 381,000, and an average annual income of $19,786 per family, Brevard is expected to top half a million people by the year 2000. If pioneers like Captain Burnham and John Houston were to return today, they would find it difficult to recognize old "Mosquito County" in this densely populated, modern, and highly developed strip of land along the Indian River. Would they believe this was once the harsh, isolated rural area they settled?

Today, Brevard County boasts 8,000 hotel rooms, 1,400 restaurants, 70 public schools with 47,000 students, 14 libraries, 17 radio stations, and 4 television stations. Its once virgin beaches are edged with towering hotels, condos, and timeshare resorts. Its port booms with submarines, shrimpers, and cruise ships.

The Space Shuttle *Discovery* was launched in 1988, and a space station is planned for 1990. Perhaps a settlement on Mars will be realized in the next century.

Everywhere is growth, expansion, restoration, and renewal, as Brevard County looks toward the twenty-first century.

The residents of Brevard take advantage of the exceptional lifestyle the county provides. This couple enjoys an afternoon of sun and fishing on the jetties of Port Canaveral. Photo by Ed Malles

At the Visitors Information Center, at Spaceport USA, full-scale replicas of missiles are on view. It is the third most popular attraction in Florida. Photo by Ron Lindsey

Clothed in traditional fashion, this Seminole Indian woman deftly sews the finishing touches on a colorful hat. Photo by Timothy O'Keefe/Southern Stock Photos

The First Georgianna Church of Merritt Island was founded in 1886. Services and Sunday school are still held each week. Photo by Ron Lindsey

The Sebastian Beach Inn, a seafood restaurant on State Road A1A near Sebastian Inlet, was once a coastal watch station during World War II. Photo by Ron Lindsey

A net fisherman on Merritt Island makes his cast into a creek. Fishing is a big part of life in Brevard County. Photo by Ron Lindsey

Cocoa resident Johnny Jones sells mangoes from a colorful fruit stand on South Tropical Trail on Merritt Island. Photo by Ron Lindsey

Rockledge celebrated its centennial in 1987. The McEwen House on Rockledge Drive is one of the oldest homes in the riverside community. Photo by Ron Lindsey

The Starship Royale, part of the Premiere Cruise Fleet, leaves Port Canaveral en route for a three-day trip to the Bahamas. Photo by Ron Lindsey

Cocoa Beach, famous for being the home of astronauts, has developed into a prosperous and attractive oceanside community. Photo by Ed Malles

A Florida Heron, one of many bird species found in Brevard County, perches on Mather's Bridge in Indian Harbour Beach as the full moon rises in the background. Photo by Ron Lindsey

The Indian River offers many spectacular scenes, such as this picturesque dock silhouetted against the falling light. Photo by Tony Arruza/Southern Stock Photos

May Day celebrations were held annually in the Titusville city park. This 1928 photo shows Titusville Elementary School children performing the Maypole Dance. This May Day event was sponsored by winter resident Dr. Helen Mack Welch. Courtesy, Bob Hudson

Once the lonely refuge of herons and alligators, today's Space Coast resounds to the rumble of rockets shooting skyward and is the epitome of the primeval paradise gently coexisting with space-age industry.

While the Space Coast is becoming ever more famous for its high-technology industries, it also enjoys a splendid reputation as a tourist mecca with white sand beaches, proximity to central Florida attractions, and a thriving cruise industry.

The main source of revenue for early Brevard residents was recovery work from ships that had foundered off the Cape Canaveral Shoals and further south on coral reefs just offshore. With nineteenth-century settlers taking advantage of the fine climate and natural abundance to be found along the Space Coast, fishing and farming became the main income-producing industries in a still undeveloped county.

From the turn of the century and well into the 1940s it looked as if citrus would become the main industry of the future. Still the area remained relatively undeveloped, with no real highways to haul goods. The county remained known as a sleepy stop on U.S. 1 between the North and Miami. Ferries delivered goods from the mainland to Merritt Island and to the beaches. There were drawbridges to Merritt Island and to the beaches as late as 1960.

The space program changed everything overnight. Once it was determined that Cape Canaveral was the ideal place from which to shoot rockets in the early 1950s, Brevard County was inundated with scientists, engineers, and their support teams—every type of employee imaginable. It was a frenetic time; developers and merchants scrambled to meet the demands of hundreds of people pouring into the county nearly every week. The press, excited by the possibilities the space program engendered, fanned the flames. Everything grew, nearly out of control. People came to love the gentle county with its perfect climate and myriad natural resources.

It was quite a blow when the space program was severely cut back in the early 1970s at the end of the Apollo Moon Program. The county survived by attracting other high-technology industries and by taking advantage of its natural resources.

Today the space program is as strong as ever, the renewed utilization of the space shuttle contributing to the area's success and growth. Brevard County has built up its other industries to achieve a broad, flourishing base of prosperity. The future for the Space Coast looks sunny and successful.

The organizations whose stories appear here have chosen to support this important literary and civic project. They illustrate the variety of ways in which individuals and their businesses and organizations have contributed to making the area an excellent place to live, work, and visit.

COCOA BEACH AREA CHAMBER OF COMMERCE

Above: Brevard Avenue in Cocoa Village during the 1940s; at that time the cities of Cocoa, Rockledge, Merritt Island, and Cocoa Beach each had their own individual chambers.

Above right: The Merritt Island office of the Cape Kennedy Area Chamber of Commerce housed the Better Business Division during the early 1970s.

The Cocoa Beach Area Chamber of Commerce is a vital network of business people working for local citizens, their businesses, and the community. This chamber is made up of five communities: Cocoa Beach, Cape Canaveral, Merritt Island, Rockledge, and Cocoa. In 1921 the cities of Cocoa, Rockledge, and Merritt Island founded their own individual chambers. Cocoa Beach followed suit in 1925.

On September 1, 1968, these individual chambers of commerce merged into the Cape Kennedy Area Chamber of Commerce with offices maintained in each of the areas.

Below: Chamber volunteer Theresa Johnson stirs seafood gumbo during the annual Port Canaveral Seafood Festival hosted since 1984 by the Cocoa Beach Area Chamber of Commerce, the Canaveral Port Authority, and the local seafood industry.

The Industrial Development Division was administered at the Cocoa-Rockledge office, the Better Business Bureau was located at the Merritt Island facility, and the Tourism and Convention Division was handled at the Cocoa Beach office.

During 1975 it was proposed to change the name of the Cape Kennedy Area Chamber of Commerce to the Cocoa Beach Area Chamber of Commerce in order to better reflect the area's identification. "Seven years after the consolidation of the chambers, sectionalism was virtually nonexistent. We were united as one chamber with the purpose of effectively serving Central Brevard," commented past president Tommy Alston.

Due to substantial growth it was determined in 1982 that a new chamber facility was needed. The 4,000-square-foot building was completed in 1984 and is located at the corner of Fortenberry Road and Plumosa Street on Merritt Island. Board members and past presidents completed a successful fund-raising drive for the construction of the new facility. The chamber's former office at 431 Riveredge Boulevard in Cocoa was built 30 years ago through a similar volunteer effort.

Bannered as one of Florida's premier seafood festivals, the Port Canaveral Seafood Festival has been hosted since 1984 by the Cocoa Beach Area Chamber of Commerce, the Canaveral Port Authority, and the local seafood industry. More than 50,000 people from all over Florida attend this seafood extravaganza held the last weekend in March. Festivities include a seafood smorgasbord, nonstop entertainment, community exhibits, tours aboard naval vessels, and much more.

Presently, the Cocoa Beach Area Chamber of Commerce boasts more than 1,500 members and supports 20 task forces, or committees, which range from Government Affairs to Communications and Marketing. The chamber is also comprised of three councils: the Economic Development Council, Better Business Council, and Tourism and Convention Council.

Historically, the Cocoa Beach Area Chamber of Commerce has consisted of a vital network of business people working together to constantly upgrade the quality of life in the area and to make Central Brevard the best it can be. "The outlook for the future is an even stronger chamber with continued efforts of stimulating business, expanding markets, and increasing profits into the twenty-first century," concludes Larry Malta, chamber executive vice-president.

FLORIDA TODAY

Left: Inside Gannett Plaza, the main hallway, known as the Company Street, stretches 422 feet, connecting the production facilities at the north of the building to the front entrance at the south end. The curved glass archway provides natural lighting.

Above: Looking northwest from the edge of U.S. Highway 1, the new Gannett Plaza complex rests on 28 well-manicured acres that feature two man-made lakes as part of the irrigation and drainage system.

FLORIDA TODAY, one of America's few new newspapers, has been a jet-propelled success story since it was launched on the Space Coast more than two decades ago. Originally called TODAY, the paper was renamed on August 26, 1985, to reflect its colorful new makeup.

The paper was founded by Gannett Co., Inc., and chairman Allen H. Neuharth on March 21, 1966, to give Brevard County its own daily and Sunday-morning newspaper. The new publication zoomed to 30,000 subscribers in the first two months. Since then its circulation has nearly tripled.

The paper's success was no accident. Long before its launch, Neuharth, then Gannett's executive vice-president, made two key moves: He and other company executives worked out a proposal to purchase the long-established and respected Cocoa Tribune, an afternoon daily owned by the late Marie Holderman that served the Central Brevard area. Gannett's position in the community was later strengthened when the voice of North Brevard—the Titusville Star-Advocate—joined the company, along with the former Eau Gallie Courier in South Brevard. Second, Neuharth commissioned national pollster Louis Harris to do a complete survey of the area to determine what Space Coast readers wanted in a newspaper.

Neuharth and a team of experts designed a completely new newspaper—tailored specifically to meet the needs of Space Coast residents. It was little wonder that TODAY, with its bright headlines, large photos, innovative layout, and attention to local detail, was an instant hit with readers.

It also had a heavy impact in the journalism community, winning numerous national and state awards in its first year—especially for its coverage of the Apollo launch pad fire in January 1967 that killed three astronauts. The paper has gained solid credentials in the years since, winning hundreds of newspaper writing and design awards, and was a finalist in the Pulitzer Awards competition for photographic coverage of the January 1986 Space Shuttle Challenger explosion.

Many of the lessons learned during the startup of TODAY were put to practical use again in the early 1980s by Neuharth and the Gannett Co. in creating the highly successful national newspaper, USA TODAY.

Starting with a handful of employees in the former Tribune building on Forrest Avenue in Cocoa, FLORIDA TODAY has become one of Brevard County's major employers with some 500 on the payroll. The newspaper outgrew its original location, moving to a modern new facility at Gannett Plaza in the Suntree area of North Melbourne.

The modern steel-and-glass structure is situated on 28 acres of carefully landscaped grounds facing U.S. 1 and the Indian River. The huge production facility contains two complete new press lines, which can print FLORIDA TODAY and USA TODAY simultaneously. Brevard has been a USA TODAY print site since 1985, supplying papers to Central and North Florida and South Georgia. The production and office facilities at Gannett Plaza feature the latest state-of-the-art equipment, from the mailroom to the newsroom.

A huge dish antenna outside the front entrance to the main office building is used to receive USA TODAY pages by satellite for printing and distribution. Also greeting visitors as they enter the building is a bust of the paper's founder. Etched into the marble base is a quotation from Neuharth's 1966 introductory message that remains the paper's number-one commitment: "TODAY's goal is to preserve the best traditions of this historic birthplace of the Space Age and to help ensure its bright tomorrow."

RON JON SURF SHOP

The huge complex that is now Ron Jon Surf Shop was started under Ron DiMenna's porch in Manahawkin, New Jersey. DiMenna, an avid surfer, figured that if he purchased two boards at a good price, he could sell one and make enough profit to allow him to keep the second one. Instead he ended up selling both boards, and a business was born. He bought five more boards and sold those.

Over the past 25 years the Ron Jon Surf Shop has grown remarkably and now includes everything from the original surfboards to casual clothing and kites. The business has contributed greatly to the success of Cocoa Beach as a recreation area.

DiMenna was soon ordering his boards by the tractor-trailer load. He started selling from the tractor-trailer on Long Beach Island in New Jersey—not far from the surf. The entrepreneur chose the name Ron Jon because he liked the way Jon rhymed with Ron. That was in 1963.

That same year DiMenna came to Brevard County and liked what he saw: The surf was good, the physical geography was similar to Long Beach Island, and his business instincts (which seem to have been working overtime already) told him Cocoa

In the process of expansion the firm donated parking and the inherent landscaping of a park to the City of Cocoa Beach. The expanded two-story building stands in the heart of the city, flanked by an oasis of greenery and the Atlantic Ocean.

Ron Jon, which now offers much more than surfboards, says it sells "fun in the sun," which includes everything from surfboard wax to diving equipment to casual clothing. This is reflected in the number of employees on board: The store started out with three employees; now it employs 180.

The people at Ron Jon Surf Shop know they were in the right place and made the right moves at the right time. They were largely instrumental in Brevard County becoming recognized as the leader on the East Coast for beach wear and the surfing industry as a whole. As surfing and water sports have grown in popularity, so has Ron Jon; it has always kept pace with the demands of this growth industry.

Beach was a great place to locate a surf shop.

The first Ron Jon Surf Shop was quite small and located in front of the pier in Cocoa Beach, on A-1-A. As the business again took off (a matter of months), more room was needed—and the shop was moved to Third Street and North Orlando Avenue, remaining there until 1967. Again bursting at the seams, the shop was relocated to its present facility at 4151 North Atlantic Avenue in Cocoa Beach.

The new shop started out with an impressive 3,000 square feet. By 1976 it had grown to encompass 4,500 square feet. As the surfing industry continued to grow, so did the store. In 1983 it nearly doubled its size, to 8,700 square feet. In 1986 the store was 17,000 square feet; then it was decided that still further expansion was necessary. Today Ron Jon Surf Shop is a beautiful and majestic 37,500 square feet, with the owner already giving consideration to future expansion.

DAVIES & HOUSER

The Davies & Houser building, located close to historic downtown Cocoa, Florida.

With tax law and financial markets in constant flux, a company's potential for success is enhanced to a great extent by its accounting firm. The accounting firm must be able to understand the company's financial goals and work with management to develop creative strategies to achieve them.

For many years the accounting firm of Davies & Houser has provided a wide range of tax, accounting, management, and advisory services for numerous Brevard County businesses ranging from large health care organizations and city agencies to small and mid-size retailers, construction firms, and manufacturing companies. Regardless of size, Davies & Houser clients can expect a multiservice approach tailored to their immediate needs and anticipated future goals.

Davies & Houser's many tax services include tax return preparation, tax planning to minimize future tax obligations, audit representation, and estate planning. Clients are advised on the tax implications of starting, buying, selling, or liquidating a business. Tax shelters, employee benefits, retirement plans, and incorporation procedures are examined for possible inclusion in the client's long-range business plans. The firm also counsels executives on an individual basis concerning their income and estate tax planning.

Davies & Houser provides tax reporting services, financial statements, internal accounting analysis, inventory control, profit and cash-flow projections, and bookkeeping and payroll services. The firm's wide range of experience affords clients valuable advice in many aspects of business operations. For the new or small business, Davies & Houser offers counseling on start-up formation, business and financial plans, purchase of computer systems, and assistance in obtaining capital and loan financing. The larger established company can use Davies & Houser for cash-flow planning, budgeting, installing new management information systems, investigating cases of suspected fraud, and counseling on a wide range of major business decisions.

Dan R. Davies and Wesley H. Houser founded the firm in 1972. Davies, a native Floridian, began practicing in Brevard County in 1955. He is a community leader, holding posts as a board member of the Brevard Achievement Center and Cocoa Kiwanis Club, a former director of Sun Bank of Cocoa, and a current trustee of the Florida Baptist Association.

Wesley H. Houser, also born and raised in Florida, graduated from the University of Florida and was employed with a national CPA firm before forming Davies & Houser. Among his many civic contributions, Houser has served as vice-president and treasurer of the Canaveral Port Authority, chairman of the board of Wuesthoff Hospital, president of the Cocoa Beach Area Chamber of Commerce, and chairman of the Brevard County United Way campaign.

Davies & Houser has helped many businesses in Brevard County become more profitable. The firm has grown as well: From three employees in 1972, Davies & Houser now employs a staff of nearly 20. New personnel typically go through a rigorous training program that covers the latest accounting techniques and tax regulations. The firm is headquartered in newly remodeled offices located at 535 Delannoy Avenue in the historic Cocoa Village district.

Davies & Houser will continue to provide innovative solutions to complex tax, accounting, and business problems using a variety of strategies and tools. In these uncertain, ever-changing economic times, Davies & Houser's clients find that approach the best assurance for success.

DBA SYSTEMS, INC.

DBA Systems, Inc., was originally founded to provide missile tracking analysis for the U.S. Department of Defense. For approximately 20 years thereafter, DBA stayed involved in the government systems area, providing hardware and software systems for the military defense industry.

DBA was incorporated in the State of Florida in January 1963 under the name D. Brown Associates, Inc., and assumed the name DBA Systems, Inc., in September 1968. Originally located in the old naval barracks at the Melbourne Airport, DBA later moved to its present location at 1135 West Nasa Boulevard in Melbourne.

During 1979 and 1980 the company went through a period of reorganization, and the present management team came into place under the direction of Howard N. Hebert, president and chief executive officer. Since then DBA has experienced phenomenal growth, spurred in part by the acquisition of another company, LogEtronics, Inc., in 1984, which put DBA in the medical imaging, remote sensing, and commercial graphic arts markets.

DBA develops and markets a variety of imaging systems for military and commercial uses. Imaging involves the use of trillions of dots to reproduce or imitate the form of a person or object using conventional photography or a computer. Most of DBA's business utilizes the ability to portray, manipulate, and interact with these dots in digit or matrix form. Basically, the systems acquire the image data, process it, and disseminate it either electrically or in hard copy form.

The company's operations combine technological expertise in digital image processing, photogrammetry (the process of making maps or scale drawings by aerial or other photography), and chemical-based film processing. DBA often functions as a systems integrator, putting together systems design and software for diverse markets and imaging applications.

DBA has a history of honing itself to offer its customers the greatest benefit and viability in their contract needs. As a consequence, it was decided in 1987 to focus on government and defense electronics markets. This decision was the stimulus that brought about the acquisition of Digital Cartographic Systems, Inc.—a move that merges digital map and cartographic data base products with DBA's imagery-based exploitation capabilities. The decision also warranted the sale of DBA's commercial business segments, LogEtronics, Inc., and Luth International.

The strength of DBA's growth pattern is evident by comparing revenues over the years: In 1963 revenues were $453,455; in 1968 they had more than tripled to $1,633,491; by 1980 revenues reached nearly $10.7 million; and in 1987 they were at an astronomical $82 million. The number of employees working for DBA has increased substantially, also: In 1980 there were only 196 people working for DBA; at last count there were 710.

Expansion in the government and defense electronics markets, especially through acquisition, has already begun, but it is greatly aided by the fact that DBA Systems, Inc., has in excess of two decades of experience in those very markets. Currently DBA's government systems contracts account for more than 70 percent of net sales, and that figure is growing rapidly.

The DBA building at 1200 South Woody Burke Road in Melbourne is headquarters for the development and marketing of various imaging systems for military and commercial use.

CANAVERAL PORT AUTHORITY

It took nearly 75 years to take the idea of a deep-water harbor at Cape Canaveral from the dream of naval strategists and local residents to an economically feasible reality. A small fishing village had grown up around the lighthouse at the cape; the villagers as well as local mariners were the first to determine that an anchorage would benefit the surrounding area.

The lee side of the Cape Canaveral shoals (which extends nearly eight miles into the Atlantic) offered haven to mariners for centuries. The U.S. Naval Department and the U.S. Coast and Geodetic Survey recommended construction of a port at Cape Canaveral in 1878.

By 1893 the U.S. Army Corps of Engineers certified that dredging of a deep-water harbor was possible. Since the harbor would have to be dug out of dry land, this would be quite a feat. But the Corps of Engineers did not recommend construction because they believed that the size of the local population was too small to support such a project once it was completed. The population had grown enough by 1939 for the Corps of Engineers to review the idea. In 1941 Brevard County learned that the engineers had recommended construction to Congress, with an appropriation of $1.661 million. Dredging of the harbor was scheduled to begin in 1942, however, it was delayed by World War II. It was another seven years before work actually began.

In the Rivers and Harbors Act of 1945, Congress authorized port construction. However, the year 1946 saw the Army Corps of Engineers again file an adverse report on the harbor, and then changing their minds and reporting on the project favorably. That same year Congress finally voted approval for the project, with an appropriation of $830,000 and $45,000 yearly for maintenance, with the provision that local interests match the $830,000 for the dredg-

Top right: The opening of Port Canaveral in November 1953.

Left: Port Canaveral's prolific seafood industry—including Calico Scallops pictured here—produced a wholesale value of $60 million in 1987.

Bottom right: Jetty Park, a 35-acre recreational facility located within the port proper, features campgrounds affording views of ships entering and leaving the port.

ing. After a referendum in 1947, the Canaveral Harbor Board sold $1.365 million in revenue bonds for use with matching funds for construction of the port's waterways, and for purchase of land, port improvements, and operations.

Finally, on June 26, 1950, a dredge started cutting a path from the Inland Waterway at the middle of the Indian River to the east across Merritt Island and the Banana River. Some say it was one of the

few harbors dug from the inside out. Most of the dredge spoil was used to construct a causeway across the Indian and Banana rivers for road access from the port to the mainland. In October 1951 the waters of the Atlantic mingled with the Indian River to form the Canaveral Harbor, consisting of one turning basin and a channel to the ocean.

The Port District was reorganized by the Florida Legislature in 1953 to provide for the port to be governed by an elected board of commissioners that had the right of way to levy ad valorem taxes on the electorate to finance expansion and operations.

With the way to the ocean now open to virgin fishing grounds, fishing boats were the first to use the port extensively. Leases for wharves were granted and fishing companies began erecting processing plants. A 400-foot wharf (now the West Marginal Wharf) for oceangoing vessels and crash boat stations for the Air Force missile test center were built next.

By 1955 the first ship was served, and shortly thereafter, a storm partially filled in the channel. Jetties were added in 1957 to both sides of the entrance to the channel to prevent sand erosion. This improvement ensured that the port was usable for ocean transportation.

The Canaveral Port Authority continued development of Port Canaveral through the use of revenue bonds, but development was slow. While the first cargo, European cement, had come through the port in 1955, it was not until nearly 10 years later that cargo such as lumber, more cement, petroleum, and citrus enabled the port to start paying its own way. At times, members of the authority signed personal notes to keep up the interest payments on the

Top: Scrap metal is exported from Port Canaveral to countries worldwide.

Florida citrus exported from Port Canaveral is a commodity in high demand both nationally and internationally.

Port Canaveral in 1967.

bonds. Today Port Canaveral counts its cargo in the millions of tons, handling such diverse commodities as lumber, newsprint, citrus, oil, scrap, solar salt, and many others.

The first turning basin covered approximately 100 acres and was 27 feet deep. The channel, which was also 27 feet deep, connected this turning basin to the ocean and the coastal shipping lanes nine miles to the east. West of the basin was the Barge Canal, the Banana River, and the Indian River, which was part of the Intracoastal Waterway. To connect these water systems, locks were required to compensate for the differences in elevation. Since the port authority lacked funds to construct the locks, the Barge Canal's eastern end where it joined the port was filled in.

Between 1950 and 1960 there was a tremendous surge of growth in Brevard that affected the port. When the dredging began in 1950, Brevard's population was 23,563; by 1960 it was at 111,176—a 370-percent increase. Cement and lumber were increasing drastically as primary cargoes coming through the port, and most of it went into local building.

In 1957 the land to the north side of the channel and the north and east sides of the turning basin were ceded to the federal government for use with the Atlantic Long-Range Missile Proving Ground, now the Cape Canaveral Air Force Station and the Kennedy Space Center.

Port-of-entry status was granted to Port Canaveral in 1961 by the Treasury Department. This permitted foreign vessels to add Port Canaveral to their list of ports of call and set the stage for the later emergence of the cruise industry. In 1962 Congress authorized construction of a second turning basin and the long-sought-after locks to connect the port to inland waterways.

Interestingly, the locks were constructed larger and wider than originally planned to provide for passage of the first stage of the Saturn rocket needed to put the Apollo spacecraft into orbit for manned space flight. The locks were completed by 1965; the West Turning Basin was outlined by a dike and partially dredged at that time; and a highway and deeper entrance channel were added for military requirements.

In the 1970s the military dredged a third turning basin, called the Trident Submarine Basin. The entrance channel was dredged to 46 feet, and the Canaveral Port Authority added modern wharves on the south and north sides of the port. Between 1983 and 1985 the port authority added three cruise ship terminals and a roll-on/roll-off ramp for cargo. In 1986 and 1987 two more cargo berths were added.

Port Canaveral has emerged as one of the nation's leading cruise ports and has gained worldwide recognition as the port that delivers the likes of Disney World, Sea World, and Kennedy Space Center to hundreds of thousands of visitors yearly. In 1987 three home-ported cruise ships and 12 ports of call brought 728,886 revenue passengers to Port Canaveral, making it the third-largest passenger-volume port in the country. Passenger count is expected to surpass one million by 1990.

For many years Port Canaveral partially relied on local taxes to build the piers, roads, warehouses, and other basic structures needed to attract business. By 1986 the port had increased its financial strength to the point that it was self-supporting. That year the Canaveral Port Authority generated a net operating income exceeding $2.9 million, and the board of commissioners voted unanimously to eliminate ad valorem taxes and to depend on income from user fees to fund continued development. Thus, Port Canaveral became self-supporting entirely on October 1, 1986.

Port Canaveral is now continuing to develop to serve the Brevard County community by using the surplus of user fees over expenses, which amounts to approximately $3 million per year.

When Port Canaveral was first conceived as mainly a citrus port, no one had any idea that it would grow to be so diversified in its cruise, cargo, and land-use markets. Port Canaveral has come a long way and has overcome many obstacles to be the successful, self-supporting, and profitable port that it is today.

SEAESCAPE LIMITED

SeaEscape, Florida's popular one-day cruises, are offered from Port Canaveral, Fort Lauderdale, Miami, and Tampa Bay. The popularity of SeaEscape can be attributed to the fact that it offers all the amenities of a longer cruise in just one Florida sun-filled day.

SeaEscape Limited makes it the company's business to pack as much fun, sun, and activity into each day's cruise as is humanly possible to enjoy. The idea, which incorporates everything from professional entertainment to swimming pools to delicious food, has been so successful because the price accompanying these cruises is less than $100, and the cruises can fit into just about anyone's schedule, including half-day "sampler" cruises. The popular cruises have attracted Floridians and tourists alike.

The history of SeaEscape goes back to Scandinavian World Cruises, which was founded in 1981 utilizing a car ferry concept. Scandinavian had operated the M/S Scandinavia between New York and Freeport, the M/S Scandinavian Sun between Miami and Freeport, and the Scandinavian Sky between Port Canaveral and Freeport and on cruises to nowhere. The principal business of Scandinavian World Cruises was to transport passengers and their cars on Scandinavia from New York to Florida, transferring at Freeport to the Sun or Sky, depending on passengers' ultimate destination of choice. Star Cruises Limited was formed with M/S Scandinavian Star in Tampa in 1984.

The first ship, Scandinavian Sky, was inaugurated in 1982 to operate out of Port Canaveral (it is no longer a SeaEscape vessel). The Scandinavian Sun joined the fleet in 1982 to operate out of Miami. The third ship, the Scandinavia, began operating between New York and Freeport in 1982. The following year the Scandinavia was redeployed. And, in 1984, the Scandinavian Star began operations out of Tampa.

In July 1985 SeaEscape Limited was formed. Since 1985, the Scandinavian Sky moved to Port Canaveral, the Scandinavian Sun moved to Fort Lauderdale, and the Scandinavian Star moved to Miami. In 1988 the newest ship in the fleet, the Scandinavian Saga, was operating out of St. Petersburg. And on June 30, 1988, SeaEscape announced the addition of the world's largest catamaran to the fleet, due in service spring, 1990.

Ivo Leon, president and chief executive officer of SeaEscape Limited.

The Scandinavian Sky sails out of Fort Lauderdale to the Bahamas, offering a full day of fun, sun, and activity.

PREMIER CRUISE LINES, LTD.

Only one ship in the world has Minnie Mouse as its official sponsor, and that ship is the Star/Ship *Oceanic*, owned and operated by Premier Cruise Lines, Ltd.

Premier, a subsidiary of the Greyhound Corporation, was founded in 1983 by Bruce Nierenberg and Bjornar Hermansen to offer affordable cruises to the Bahamas from Port Canaveral. The choice of Port Canaveral was natural, taking into account its proximity to Orlando, all the Central Florida attractions, and Cocoa Beach.

In March 1984 Premier's Star/Ship *Royale* sailed on her inaugural voyage and began offering year-round three- and four-day cruises to the Bahamas. In November of the following year the young cruise line was named the Official Cruise Line of Walt Disney World, and announced the purchase of its second vessel, the Star/Ship *Oceanic*, one of the largest cruise ships in the world.

The rapid growth and success of the company was due to the innovative ideas of its founders, who introduced one of the most successful vacation packages ever offered: The Cruise and Walt Disney World Vacation Week. The package, nicknamed the Magic Vacation Combination, includes a three- or four-night cruise on one of Premier's ships to the Bahamas and a three- or four-day visit to the Walt Disney World Vacation Kingdom, with a seven-day rental car, deluxe hotel accommodations, unlimited admission three-day Walt Disney World Passport, and tour of NASA's *Spaceport* USA all included free.

At the renaming ceremonies for the Star/Ship *Oceanic*, where Minnie Mouse herself acted as sponsor, Bruce Nierenberg, executive vice-president of the line, spoke of the two goals the founders had set when they formed the company in 1983. The first was to put ships into service that would be the clear-cut leaders in product superiority in all main categories of measurement: food, entertainment, passenger service, hotel operations, and itineraries. The second was to combine a deluxe cruise experience with a high-quality Walt Disney World vacation package that works. Nierenberg said, "We have met both goals. Premier Cruise Lines, with its *Royale* and *Oceanic*, is recognized, even by her competitors, as being the most deluxe in the market."

This statement gained even more credibility in 1987, when Premier Cruise Lines won the prestigious Grand Prix Mondial de Voyage as the Cruise Line of the Year from the World Travel Award Committee.

In addition to being a national leader in the tourism industry, Premier has had tremendous economic impact on Brevard County. The company employs more than 250 people in its shoreside offices alone. And, with all of its passengers spending from one to three days in the Brevard area, either visiting *Spaceport* USA or enjoying the beautiful oceanfront, Premier Cruise Lines, Ltd., promises to continue to be a positive force in the county's growth.

Top(from left): J.P. Miquel, president and chief executive officer; Captain Hook; Bruce Nierenberg, executive vice-president and co-founder; Minnie Mouse, official sponsor of the Star/Ship Oceanic; Bjornar Hermansen, executive vice-president and co-founder; Captain D. Chilas, master of the Star/Ship Oceanic; and Mickey Mouse.

Left: The Star/Ship Royale and the Star/Ship Oceanic of Premier Cruise Lines, the Official Cruise Line of Walt Disney World.

KMD SHIP REPAIR

When Kurt E. Ronstrom left his native Sweden at age 16 to be a sailor, his uncle told him, "No one in this family has ever been a sailor, and no Ronstrom will ever be a sailor."

Ronstrom not only served in the Swedish Merchant Marine and Navy for nine years, but went on to make a life for himself close to the sea.

Oliver W. "Buddy" Street, on the other hand, served in the United States Navy and took that experience into his civilian jobs in ship repair, where he eventually became ship foreman for Kurt Ronstrom. When Ronstrom started his second ship repair company, KMD Ship Repair, Street went with him as partner.

Early in his career Ronstrom had settled in Miami, where he worked for Broward County during the day and repaired small yachts at night. He founded Kurt's Marine Diesel (KMD) in 1968. His first shop in Fort Lauderdale was started with very few assets and was small enough to be accommodated in a storage shed. Still, it was his Swedish determination and his training as a diesel engineer that helped propel him to success.

By 1974 the shed facilities were no longer adequate; a new shop was built, and Kurt's Marine Diesel was incorporated. The company had long since graduated to working on cargo and cruise ships.

Seeing an opportunity for expansion, Ronstrom decided to move to Port Canaveral because of its outstanding growth pattern. He sold Kurt's Marine to an employee, Franco Licenzi, and started KMD Ship Repair of Cape Canaveral, Inc. It was at this point that Buddy Street became his partner.

The move to Port Canaveral was inspired in part by contracts to service Navy ships. Meanwhile, KMD continued to extend its services to cargo and cruise vessels. KMD has continued to be headquartered in Port Canaveral and has opened an adjunct office back in Fort Lauderdale. The firm also has a complete mobile machine and welding shop in a van so that personnel can travel to any location 24 hours a day, seven days a week to perform repair services. The skilled staff can carry out repairs at sea as well as on the pier, and the van can be loaded by crane right onto the ship.

KMD Ship Repair does everything from refurbishing cabins to hull repair, plumbing, engines, deck tiles, and rebabbitting (the application of a soft metal to reduce friction in bearings).

The company that started off with one man working out of a storage shed now has a staff of 30 and is worth more than $2 million. According to Ronstrom, "It wasn't a giant leap, it was a lot of little steps."

Kurt E. Ronstrom (left) and Oliver W. Street, Jr., owners of KMD Ship Repair of Cape Canaveral, Inc.

PORT CANAVERAL TOWING INC.

Battler was the name of the first commercial tugboat to work in Port Canaveral. It came to the port in 1958 and was owned by the newly created Port Canaveral Towing Inc., a subsidiary of Port Everglades Towing Company.

According to Bob Santos, vice-president/towing operations and marine personnel, "We believed the potential (at Port Canaveral) was obvious." It was obvious because the space program was just under way, and ships would be coming through the port carrying materials for the space industry. It was "a little slow in the beginning," according to Santos. "She sat for 60 days without turning a screw, but we weren't discouraged." Later that year *Battler* was in full operation, and plans were already being made for the delivery of a second tug.

Both Port Everglades Towing and Port Canaveral Towing are owned by parent company Hvide Shipping, Inc. Hans J. Hvide, the firm's founder, emigrated from his native Norway before World War II and had many years of shipping experience that he brought with him when he incorporated in 1958. It was Hvide who met with George J. King, the port manager at the time, to discuss tug service and Port Canaveral's future.

Hvide Shipping is notable for two industry innovations: the roll-on/roll-off ramp, better known as ro/ro, for loading cargo, and the CATUG, which is a catamaran-hulled tugboat that links and unlinks with a barge. The CATUG acts as a ship at sea yet frees the crew and tug for other work while the barge is being loaded or unloaded.

Hvide established Cape Canaveral Services Company in 1962 to provide general marine support for the Army, Navy, Air Force, and NASA at Cape Canaveral. Hvide's personnel were qualified and trained to retrieve manned space capsules and provide standby emergency retrieval support to the Mercury, Gemini, and Apollo programs. Hvide has retrieved solid and liquid rocket boosters, as well as classified satellites, warheads, and missile components in conjunction with Trident, Poseidon, Titan, Pershing, and other missile programs.

Originally Port Canaveral Towing had a contract with the Air Force, providing much needed retrieval support for the space program. But the company grew so large that it no longer qualified for the contract, which was set aside for small businesses, and the contract ended in 1983.

Today the tugs of Port Canaveral Towing Inc. do a thriving business and are kept busy with the many cargo and cruise ships that ply the Port Canaveral waters.

Thirty years ago Battler, *the first commercial tugboat to work in Port Canaveral, was owned by the newly created Port Canaveral Towing Inc.*

PORT CANAVERAL

The future looks exceedingly bright for the continued development of Port Canaveral's resources. Currently Port Canaveral owns approximately 747 acres of land above sea level. Of those, 197 acres are leased to tenants whose businesses are dependent upon or enhanced by their proximity to the harbor. Two parks in the port proper total 38 acres to meet the recreational needs of county residents. The local populace may also enjoy swimming, fishing, camping, and boating. Four double-wide boat ramps and 4.5 acres of beachfront are also open to the public, giving Port Canaveral more recreational acreage than all the other ports in Florida combined.

With the completion of the West Turning Basin in 1987, Port Canaveral has three turning basins, an entrance channel 46 feet deep, and an inner reach channel 41 feet deep. The port presently has eight cargo berths, three cruise berths, and two tanker berths. The military also has developed five deep-draft and two shallow-draft berths. The Cape Canaveral Air Force Station makes up approximately the northeast 25 percent of the port. This land is entirely controlled and zoned by the military.

Port Canaveral has a tremendous economic impact on Brevard County and Central Florida. It takes more than 5,000 people to fill the jobs created by the port. The great diversity of jobs in Port Canaveral helps to stabilize the sometimes roller-coaster economy of the county, which is dependent on the space industry and high-technology companies for much of its growth. In fact, the port's cargo, cruise, fishing, military, business, boat building, and recreational industries had an annual impact on the county in 1987 of nearly a half-billion dollars, and this number is ever increasing. Development of Port Canaveral's foreign trade zone will create more than 200 local jobs and make the port more attractive for international business.

The cargo industry alone is currently responsible for bringing in $130 million to the local area, and the cruise industry brings in another $240 million per year. A prolific fishing industry produces $60 million to $70 million in wholesale value, and military shipping activities produce another $25 million.

The port is projecting a total operating revenue for the 1989 and 1990 fiscal year of more than $9 million, and for the 1991-1992 fiscal year a total operating revenue of $13.725 million.

As the tourist industry continues to grow in Central Florida, so will Port Canaveral's cruise business. And, as more and more people move to Brevard County, there will be an ever-increasing demand for cargo coming through Canaveral's harbor. The potential for growth is impressive and nearly unlimited. The land now owned by the port can ultimately be developed into more than 60 ship berths. This activity at the port and port revenues will have a direct effect on the economy of Brevard County.

In the coming years Port Canaveral will continue to develop its resources and widen the gap between its humble beginnings as a citrus, shrimp, and oil port, and its future as a cruise and cargo port of international renown.

Port Canaveral today.

Port Canaveral's three home-ported cruise ships (left to right): SeaEscape LTD's Scandinavian Sky, *and Premier Cruise Lines'* Star/Ship Oceanic *and* Star/Ship Royale.

MID-FLORIDA FREEZERS

Mid-Florida Freezers, which has its main operation in Port Canaveral with adjunct offices in Leesburg and Plymouth, is a huge complex of temperature-controlled warehouses for the specific purpose of storing perishables such as fruit and other products that need protection from the elements.

The company started with one warehouse and big ideas. The original warehouse in Port Canaveral was part of the citrus industry and was owned by Tropicana, the fruit juice company. In 1975 Pat Lee, who is the general partner in charge of all operations, acquired the warehouse from Tropicana, which had relocated, and started the operation from scratch.

Lee is a man of much energy, and over the years he has been an active public servant in Brevard County—first as the fire chief of Cape Canaveral and now as its mayor.

That original 60,000-square-foot warehouse was outfitted with all new refrigeration capability, and Mid-Florida Freezers was officially in business. The first products stored and shipped from the warehouse were orange juice, in the form of Brazilian concentrate stored in 55-gallon drums, and imported meat—frozen beef and lamb.

By 1982 the company had also acquired a special 90,000-square-foot concrete building designed to store newsprint. The newsprint that is stored by Mid-Florida is utilized by paper publishers the length and breadth of the state, from the *St. Petersburg Times, Orlando Sentinel, Florida Today, USA Today,* and Cape Publishing in Central Florida to Okaloosa in the panhandle and Boca Raton in the south. A full shipload of 8,500 tons of newsprint comes through the warehouse every three to four weeks.

Today Mid-Florida Freezers no longer handles imported meat, but it still handles citrus products and stores grapefruit for export. It also stores lumber and steel as well as newsprint. Products are shipped from Mid-Florida warehouses to as far away as Germany and Japan.

Mid-Florida Freezers as it looked in 1975, when the firm was founded.

From a small warehouse operation Mid-Florida Freezers has grown to a multimillion-dollar business.

The company provides its clients with special refrigerated warehouse facilities for the export and import of citrus products, newsprint, and storage buildings for lumber and steel.

When Mid-Florida was founded in 1975, the operation had six employees; today it has more than 65. Currently Mid-Florida Freezers has 10 warehouses in Port Canaveral, covering 35 acres in the main storage area and another 15 acres some quarter-mile west of that. The plant in Plymouth has 135,000 square feet of floor space and the one in Leesburg has 185,000 square feet. They are both conveniently located next to rail sidings. Over a 12-year period Mid-Florida Freezers has experienced phenomenal growth and has gone from a small company with one warehouse to a multimillion-dollar operation.

FAT BOYS' FRANCHISE SYSTEMS, INC.

The day Jesse Keller opened his first Fat Boy's in Cape Canaveral, he made $100; today Fat Boys' averages $27 million in annual sales.

With franchises from Columbus, Ohio, to Missouri to Nassau in the Bahamas (well in excess of 40 in all), the story of Fat Boy's rise to fame and fortune reads like a modern-day Horatio Alger story—only it is the Jesse Keller story.

After stints in the Marine Corps during World War II and the Korean War, Keller returned to his native Florida and became a Sears merchandise manager in Miami. Meanwhile his brother was operating a barbecue restaurant in Naples, Florida, and Keller picked up some barbecue experience there. While he was still working at Sears, he kept experimenting with his own small barbecue pit in his backyard. The constant experimenting resulted in a growing reputation for delicious barbecues, and he was often called on to cook for large organizations.

Finally he decided to find a good location and open his own restaurant. He opened his restaurant in 1958 using the name Fat Boy's (one that he believed was memorable, and it has proven itself to be). He chose the Space Coast because he believed it had a lot of growth potential: The space program was just getting under way then, and his choice of location proved to be as fortuitous as his choice of name.

According to Keller, there is a reason that Fat Boy's is so popular: "We built the whole concept on quality service, quality food, and good prices. There just aren't that many places you can get dinner for four for under $25." All that may be true, but there is also the matter of the fabulous Fat Boy's sauce; the priceless secret recipe that everyone craves is, well, a secret. Add to that, western grain-fed beef cooked slowly over Black Jack oak, and it adds up to an unbeatable combination.

Apparently more people think Fat Boy's is unbeatable than just sophisticated southerners. In 1987 Jesse Keller's combination of keen business sense and good cookery paid off when *Entrepreneur* magazine picked the franchise company to be in the Franchise 500 as the top barbecue franchise in the nation.

The firm started franchising restaurants in 1968 in response to demand from friends and appreciative customers. Later Jay Bradley, one of those appreciative customers, was brought in to run the franchise operation. Bradley is president and chief operating officer at Fat Boys' Franchise Systems, Inc., and Keller is chairman of the board. Today Fat Boy's employs more than 1,000 people nationwide.

While corporate headquarters are in Cocoa, Fat Boy's fame is quite extensive. Most people never forget the name, but there was the woman from Maine who could remember the sauce but not the name. She stopped at a Brevard gas station to ask directions for "Chubby Fellows'"—nevertheless, she happily found her way back to Fat Boy's.

Left: Jesse Keller, founder of Fat Boy's Bar-B-Q and chairman of the board.

Right: Jay Bradley, president and chief operating officer of Fat Boys' Franchise Systems, Inc.

W.S. BLACK COMPANY, INC.

When William S. "Bill" Black started his heating and air conditioning company in June 1960, he brought to it the winning style and determination of an Olympic athlete. This was really not so surprising since he was one. It has been this determination to succeed despite the odds that has made the W.S. Black Company the success it is today.

Black was 13th in the nation for the decathlon in the 1956 Olympic tryouts. Today, more than 30 years later, he still competes in local athletic competitions, and this willingness to stay active and fit carries over into Black's business philosophy.

Black put himself through the University of Nebraska and vocational school, graduating with the highest grade point average that Lindsay-Hopkins Vocational School in Miami had had in 10 years. After graduation Black came to Brevard County and worked for another air conditioning company before starting his own firm.

Black's background of scholastic and athletic determination and success stood him in good stead when he had to guide his business through two local depressions, which were related to employee cutbacks at Kennedy Space Center. These two economic downtrends occurred in 1973 and 1974 and again in 1984 and 1985. Dead on the heels of the first economic downtrend, the W.S. Black Company barely sur-

The W.S. Black Company specializes in servicing heating and air conditioning for both residential and commercial units, including ice machines and walk-in coolers.

vived a fire that completely destroyed the business. The fire was only part of the problem.

In 1966 Black had hired E. Ann Proctor as his bookkeeper. She relocated in 1972, and Black hired a replacement bookkeeper. That second bookkeeper embezzled enough money to nearly do the business in before Black could attribute the faulty books to her. She was prosecuted, but very little money was recovered. After that disaster Proctor returned to the company and has been its secretary/treasurer ever since.

Even with the odds at times not at all in his favor, Black has certainly triumphed. His company services heating and air conditioning units, commercial refrigeration units, ice machines, walk-in coolers, and all sorts of commercial air conditioning and refrigeration units. Its expertise includes all brands. Currently the operation that went through such painful growth pangs grosses well in excess of a half-million dollars per year. The firm, which has always been on Merritt Island, recently moved to a larger location.

The excellent reputation of the W.S. Black Company is based on its impeccable integrity. This reputation, a reflection of Black's personal integrity and determination, has carried the company through thick and thin to make it the stable success that it is today.

The W.S. Black Company was nearly destroyed by a fire in 1974, but it has since become so successful that it recently moved to larger quarters.

MORTON THIOKOL, INC.

Morton Thiokol's involvement with Brevard County started in the late 1950s, when its Hermes motor successfully launched the RVA-10 rocket from Cape Canaveral. Since that time the company, then known as Thiokol (a word formed by combining the Greek words "thio," which means sulfur, and "kol," which means glue), has been continuously involved in activities at Cape Canaveral, Kennedy Space Center, and Titusville.

Morton Thiokol has provided booster and upper-stage propulsion systems for ground and underwater launches, satellite deployment from orbiters, as well as retrorockets for recovery of research

The administrative offices of Morton Thiokol, Inc., Space Services are located in Titusville.

and reusable items. Included in the programs for which the company has provided propulsion are Minuteman, Delta, Poseidon, and Trident. In addition, more than 90 percent of all U.S.-launched satellites have been boosted by Morton Thiokol-built payload assist motors.

The firm provided retrorockets during Mercury, Gemini, and Surveyor programs—Mercury and Gemini to slow their forward motion toward the earth at the completion of their missions, and the Surveyor's forward

motion toward the moon was slowed and the landing controlled by company-manufactured retro and vernier motors. Other tasks were added when the company assumed responsibility for processing the solid rocket motors (SRMs), external tanks (ETs), and retrieval operations for the space shuttle program.

In the early 1970s Morton Thiokol opened an office at the space center as part of its role in the shuttle program. That office became responsible for hands-on processing of the SRMs during assembly (or "stacking," as the operation is called) in the Vehicle Assembly Building.

In 1982 the company merged with Morton-Norwich Products, Inc., to form Morton Thiokol, Inc. The corporate headquarters of Morton Thiokol, Inc., is located in Chicago.

In 1983 a team that included Morton Thiokol successfully bid on the contract to provide shuttle processing to NASA. With the inception of the Shuttle Processing Contract (SPC) in early 1984, Morton Thiokol's tasks increased to include receiving and off-loading SRM segments as they are received from the manufacturing site in Utah, as well as increased responsibilities during stacking operations. SPC employees also receive and off-load the ET from the barge upon which it is shipped to Kennedy Space Center from its manufacturing site. The ETs are then mated to the already stacked solid rocket booster or stored until they are required for processing for a launch. Specialized crews then assist other contractors in attaching the orbiter to the ET and SRBs on the Mobile Launcher Platform (MLP) in the Vehicle Assembly Building. After the MLP containing the SRMs, ET, and orbiter rolls out to the launch pad, specialized crews assist in prelaunch preparation there.

At the time of each launch, two retrieval ships, the *Freedom Star* and the *Liberty Star*, are stationed near the projected site where the empty solid rocket booster cases will splash into the water after being jettisoned, approximately two minutes after launch. Company divers and ships personnel secure the empty cases and prepare them for towing back to Cape Canaveral, where the retrieved cases are disassembled and returned to Utah. There the cases are refurbished for use in future launches.

The majority of the Morton Thiokol, Inc., employees in Brevard County are located at the Kennedy Space Center and Cape Canaveral Air Force Station. The administrative offices are located in Titusville.

JIM RATHMANN CHEVROLET-CADILLAC, INC.

The story of Jim Rathmann Chevrolet-Cadillac, Inc., has a very dramatic beginning. In 1960 Jim Rathmann won the Indianapolis 500. Shortly thereafter, General Motors approached him with the idea of opening a dealership and he accepted, buying out Fordyce Chevrolet in Melbourne.

When Jim Rathmann opened his Chevrolet and Cadillac dealership in 1961, the entire dealership was on one acre. Two sales people from Fordyce stayed on to work for the new dealership and are still with the company—more than 25 years later. Today the dealership is spread over 16 beautifully landscaped acres and is one of the most modern, high-tech-equipped agencies in the United States.

Over the years Rathmann has had a tremendous amount of experience with automobiles and racing. He competed in the Indianapolis 500 14 times, placing second in 1952, 1957, and 1959 before winning in 1960. He also won the 500-mile race for Indy-type cars at Monza, Italy, in 1958, and he won the only 200-mile Indy-type car race ever run at the Daytona International Speedway in 1959.

Competitive racing wasn't the only thing Jim Rathmann excelled at. From 1952 to 1962 he owned an automotive specialists company in Miami that included building marine engines and high-performance engines for General Motors Corporation and the public. After winning the Indianapolis 500, Rathmann manufactured go-carts and went on to capture the world championship two years in a row.

Since the beginning of the space program, Rathmann has maintained close ties with the astronauts. When the Moon Rover meandered its way over the moon's surface, it had a Jim Rathmann Chevrolet-Cadillac emblem on the back. In fact, when NASA put a replica of the Moon Rover on exhibition, it wrote to Rathmann and asked for another emblem so that it could be authentic in every detail. It all started when astronauts Wally Schirra and Gus Grissom, who were car buffs, came to the shop one day to meet the famous race driver. Later Chevrolet issued Corvettes to the astronauts, and Rathmann met Gordon Cooper

From left to right: Bruce Crower, chief mechanic; Gordon Cooper, astronaut; Jim Rathmann, in car; and Gus Grissom, astronaut formed GCR Racing, building an Indianapolis car that raced on the circuit for two years.

The Jim Rathmann Chevrolet-Cadillac dealership is located on 16 acres of beautifully landscaped property and is equipped with the most modern high-tech equipment available for servicing customers' cars.

and Peter Conrad; they are still good friends today.

Grissom, Cooper, and Rathmann formed GCR Racing, building an Indianapolis car that raced on the circuit for two years. Kaye, Jim Rathmann's wife, was a competitive member of the race team. After *Apollo XII* four commemorative coins with diamonds were struck; three went to the astronauts' wives and the fourth went to Kaye Rathmann.

While Rathmann is still chief executive officer of Jim Rathmann Chevrolet-Cadillac, Inc., he has turned over the reigns to his son Jimmy, who is president and general manager.

Today Jimmy Rathmann carries on the family racing tradition in his father's footsteps, but more as a hobby since the dealership demands so much of his time. Currently the dealership sells 5,000 cars per year. The Service Department was recently enlarged to increase the number of customer cars serviced per day from 140 to 250. The Parts Department houses 25,000 square feet of parts inventory.

Jimmy Rathmann admits that his father's fame has helped the business, but says that now the dealership relies heavily on its reputation for outstanding service.

GRUMMAN CORPORATION

Left: Leroy R. Grumman, one of the founders of Grumman Aircraft Engineering Corporation.

Center: The LM-5 Eagle, designed and built by Grumman, safely carried astronauts Neil Armstrong and "Buzz" Aldrin on their trip to the moon July 20, 1969.

Right: The Grumman E-8 Joint STARS aircraft that looks deep into enemy territory to give early warning of attack.

Grumman Corporation has been in Florida since 1950 but first came to the Space Coast in the 1960s to work on the Apollo program. In fact, it was Grumman technology that helped land men on the moon when, on July 20, 1969, the LM-5 Eagle, designed and built by Grumman, safely carried astronauts Neil Armstrong and "Buzz" Aldrin to the lunar surface. At the peak of the Apollo program, there were 9,000 men and women working on the Lunar Module program at Grumman, with 1,600 of them on the LM team at Kennedy Space Center.

Long before "high tech" became a fashionable term, Grumman was a high-technology company. The firm designs and integrates complex electronic systems for aircraft and spacecraft, automatic test equipment for military and commercial customers, and computer systems for business, scientific, and military applications. Grumman has integrated more different electronic systems into more different aircraft than any other company in the world.

The Grumman Aircraft Engineering Corporation (now Grumman Corporation) was established on Long Island in 1930 by six young men who left Loening Aircraft Company because it was moving from New York City. They pooled their money and opened for business in an old automobile showroom and garage at Baldwin on Long Island. The company soon outgrew those quarters and moved several times before eventually building permanent facilities at Bethpage, Long Island.

In addition to repairing seaplanes and building pontoons, Grumman began designing and building its own aircraft. Roy Grumman, for whom the company was named, was an engineering genius. He designed the first retractable landing gear for military aircraft, which helped Grumman fighter planes go 20 miles per hour faster than any other at the time. He also developed an innovative wing-fold design that dramatically saved aircraft hangar space at sea, enabling the Navy to send more planes to sea aboard its carriers.

During World War II Grumman fighters and torpedo bombers were the backbone of the Carrier Navy in the Pacific. These planes were so dependable and tough that Navy carrier pilots nicknamed Grumman "The Ironworks." By the 1960s Grumman was building highly specialized electronic systems for air and space vehicles—leading to the contract for the Lunar Module and Grumman's presence in Brevard County.

The Melbourne Systems Division of Grumman is responsible for the full-scale development of the Joint Surveillance Target Attack Radar System (Joint STARS) for the Air Force and Army. It looks deep into enemy territory to give early warning of attack. This airborne wide-area ground surveillance radar will detect, locate, classify, and track both moving and fixed objects in all weather conditions. By denying enemy forces the element of surprise, Joint STARS will increase the battle management effectiveness of allied conventional forces.

Concurrently, Grumman Technical Services at Titusville provides service, maintenance, and testing of aircraft and space vehicles, simulators, and trainers. At Kennedy Space Center, Technical Services is part of the Shuttle Processing Team and manages an elaborate network of computers and software systems used in the shuttle turnaround and launch-processing system.

When they started out, those early aircraft pioneers at Grumman had no idea what the future would bring. Their achievements, and those of the thousands who came after them, fill the chapters of a Grumman history that has spanned six decades, seen the company progress from fabric-covered aircraft to manned space flight, grow from six people to nearly 35,000, expand from a tiny garage to more than 100 manufacturing and field sites, count its annual sales in billions of dollars rather than thousands, and gain a reputation as one of the nation's foremost aerospace companies.

WUESTHOFF HEALTH SYSTEMS, INC.

Wuesthoff Hospital is quickly approaching a half-century of health care services in Brevard County, and every year marks a renewed commitment to serve the community.

While population explosions have had a major impact on the growth from a 10-bed hospital in 1941 to a 308-bed medical complex in 1988, the desire for quality care has had even greater impact. The quest for new technology, better methods, more diversified and highly trained staff, more convenience for the patient—all these factors have influenced growth to meet patient needs.

A not-for-profit community hospital, Wuesthoff was founded in 1940 by a group of area physicians who dreamed of building a community hospital in Rockledge. Led by physician Tom Kenaston and the Reverend William Hargrave, the dream was spurred

Funds to build Wuesthoff Hospital came from the heirs of longtime resident Eugene Wuesthoff, and from a community drive spearheaded by the chamber of commerce.

Wuesthoff Hospital has been serving the community since 1941, when it opened as a 10-bed facility for the people of Central Brevard.

by contributions from the heirs of longtime winter resident Eugene Wuesthoff, who also envisioned a hospital in the pleasant community by the Indian River.

The Wuesthoff gift of $12,500 came with the stipulation that an equal amount be raised by the community. With that challenge and a fund-raising campaign organized by the chamber of commerce, more than 500 people donated to the building fund.

Although they had the money, the organizers had no land until Dr. Robert Schlernitzauer came across the former golf course at the old Indian River Hotel in Rockledge. Since Dr. Bob (as he was called) was mayor of Rockledge, he influenced the city council to donate the land for the new hospital, and the dream became a reality.

The hospital opened in December 1941 with 10 beds and limited medical facilities, and treated its first patient, a young highway patrol officer injured on U.S. 1, the night before the opening.

Eugene Wuesthoff Memorial Hospital started with a staff of three physicians, one surgeon, two nurses, an orderly, a cook, and an administrator, Mildred Park. The patient census the first year was approximately 250.

Wuesthoff Hospital opened in 1941 with a small but dedicated nursing staff.

Governed by a board of directors from civic groups, business, and industry, the hospital thrived in its quest to provide the best medical care in Brevard County. From 1951 to 1978 the institution went through five separate expansion projects to meet the needs of a growing county. In 1983 Wuesthoff initiated a $35-million major expansion/renovation project to meet the community's changing needs and opened a new five-story addition in November 1986.

Today Wuesthoff Health Services, Inc. utilizes 308 beds with a medical staff of more than 150 physicians and 1,400 employees, and has reached out into the sprawling Brevard community to establish satellite medical centers, dental centers, fitness centers, hospice and home care, laboratory and diagnostic services, substance abuse programs, and complete outpatient care.

FLORIDA INSTITUTE OF TECHNOLOGY

Florida Institute of Technology is Florida's only technological university, developing highly skilled scientists, engineers, and business leaders of tomorrow.

The original mission of F.I.T. was to provide continuing education to the scientific community assembled at the nearby Kennedy Space Center. Among the early faculty were some of the space center's most learned scientists. F.I.T. has grown into a university of international standing, known for its leadership in academics and research. It stands as truly the only university of its kind in the Southeast.

F.I.T. is located in Melbourne on a tropical 146-acre campus. A coeducational, independent, fully accredited university, F.I.T. has an enrollment approaching 7,000, with students attending from throughout the world.

Students at Florida Institute of Technology work toward associate's, bachelor's, master's, and Ph.D degrees in more than 125 programs, most of them in highly technical subject areas. More than 14,000 students have earned degrees at the university since it opened its doors 30 years ago.

At the Florida Institute of Technology researchers are busy with scientific inquiries throughout the university.

F.I.T. is composed of four basic divisions—The College of Science and Engineering, The School of Management and Humanities, The School of Psychology, and The School of Aeronautics.

A number of special programs rarely found at other academic institutions are offered at Florida Institute of Technology. The Oceanography and Ocean Engineering program, established in 1972, uses the nearby Atlantic Ocean for its field of study, offering several different disciplines that include laboratory work and field trips aboard oceangoing vessels.

The need for highly qualified pilots, as well as professionals trained in business and electronic technology for the aviation industry, brought about the creation of the School of Aeronautics in 1967. Degrees are offered in aviation management, flight technology, aircraft systems management, and other areas of ground control.

F.I.T. recently created the Space Research Institute to focus on the science and engineering of space exploration to benefit programs at Kennedy Space Center. The institute will initially specialize in the areas of space flight engineering, space science research, and space enterprise research. An early focus will be on launch vehicles and space transportation.

The university has wide-ranging plans to expand and renovate its campus classrooms and laboratories, enhance its library, and add to its learned faculty. F.I.T. president Lynn Weaver is spearheading the university's first capital campaign, with the goal of raising $25 million to help F.I.T. maintain its position of leadership and academic excellence.

While the university is known for its academic intensity, students enjoy

Students heading for class through the botanical garden enjoy the tropical setting of the Melbourne campus.

a wide variety of social and recreational opportunities during their off hours, including scuba diving, drama, karate, and others. Athletic facilities on campus include two swimming pools, tennis courts, softball fields, a baseball field, soccer fields, and a gymnasium.

F.I.T.'s baseball, basketball, track, and other intercollegiate teams consistently fare well in competition. In particular, F.I.T.'s crew team has gained international attention, winning the national small college championships and competing in the prestigious Royal Henley Invitational Regatta in England.

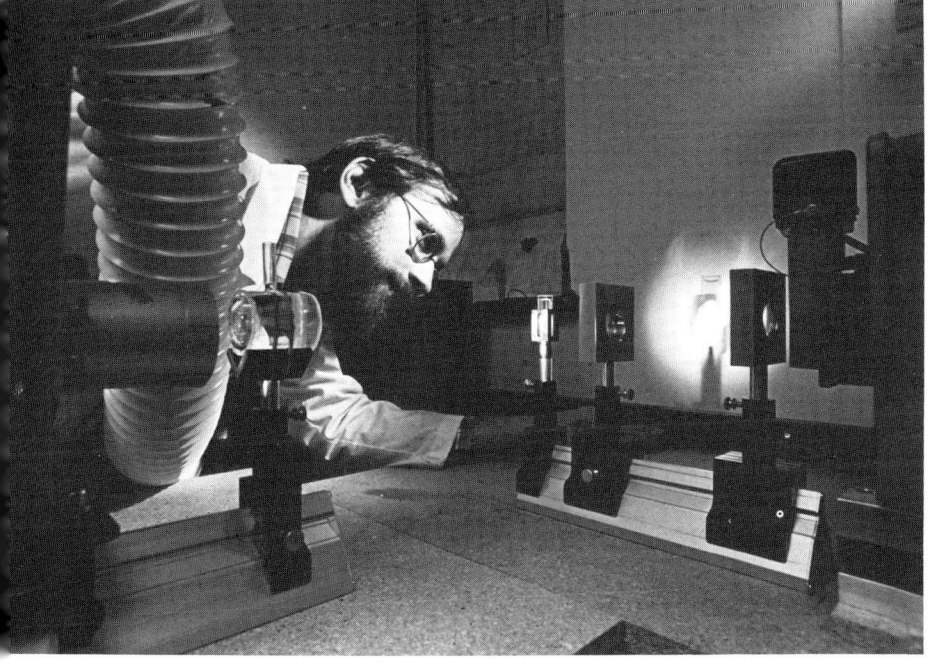

McDONNELL DOUGLAS ASTRONAUTICS COMPANY

The presence of McDonnell Douglas Astronautics Company in Brevard County is both varied and far reaching. There are three divisions that function separately from each other. The first is the McDonnell Douglas Florida Test Center at Cape Canaveral Air Force Station. The second, located at Kennedy Space Center, administers the NASA contract, the payload processor for the nation's space shuttle. The third is a missile-manufacturing facility located in the northern part of the county.

McDonnell Douglas first began business in 1920 as the Davis-Douglas Company in California, building a bi-plane called the *Cloudster*. Donald Douglas, then one of the nation's leading aeronautical engineers, developed airplanes that continued to evolve and eventually led to the famous aircraft series designation DC (Douglas Commercial). In 1939 James McDonnell founded McDonnell Aircraft Corporation in St. Louis, Missouri, and almost immediately began manufacturing airplane parts, bomber destroyers, and bomber trainers. Meanwhile, Douglas was building military aircraft. McDonnell research on the application of jet propulsion to aircraft (a new concept) had much significance for the future of the aircraft industry. The company's research led to the FH-1 Phantom, the first operational carrier-based jet and the progenitor of a long line of fighter aircraft.

Below: The McDonnell Douglas-built Gemini spacecraft undergoing tests prior to flight.

Above: The McDonnell Douglas-operated payload canister-transporter and space shuttle orbiter at Launch Pad B, Kennedy Space Center. Payloads that are installed vertically in the shuttle are placed in the payload canister, where they are transported to the orbiter for installation in the shuttle payload bay.

Almost a year before the United States announced a plan to orbit a man around the Earth, the firm's engineering team in St. Louis anticipated the need and began work on the project. The Mercury spacecraft that was chosen from the NASA competition drew praise from engineers and scientists worldwide.

The seven original astronauts followed every aspect of the Mercury spacecraft production in St. Louis. Clean rooms were established to meet the stringent standards required for the manufacturing of the spacecraft. Suborbital flights took astronauts Alan Shepard and Gus Grissom on test flights 100 miles above the earth's surface.

The Mercury spacecraft lifts off from Cape Canaveral.

Then an Atlas rocket took John Glenn and *Friendship 7* (the name of the Mercury spacecraft) into orbit on February 20, 1962.

After the Mercury proved that man could live and work in space, the Gemini spacecraft was designed by McDonnell under NASA guidelines to master the orbital environment and test the techniques that would allow man to get to the moon and back.

Even while the Gemini spacecraft were flight-testing the techniques for journeys to the moon, the hydrogen-fueled S-IVB stage rocket was being designed and tested by McDonnell Douglas. The S-IVB pushed the Apollo spacecraft into Earth orbit and then reignited to accelerate the spacecraft toward the moon.

The early history of space exploration is totally intertwined with the history of McDonnell Douglas, which resulted from the merger of its two predecessor companies in 1967.

The firm's tradition of being at the forefront of space exploration is still being carried out at Kennedy Space Center, where more than 1,300 employees perform work on the payload ground operations contract for NASA-s space shuttle. Under the separate shuttle payload operations contract with the U.S. Air Force, the Kennedy Space Center division is equally responsible for receiving, processing, and integrating Department of Defense payloads aboard the shuttle.

Also, for more than 30 years the McDonnell Douglas Florida Test Center has been the launching ground for McDonnell Douglas Thor missiles and Delta rockets. Located at the southeastern section of the Cape Canaveral Air Force Station, the area today has two active launch pads and a variety of support facilities.

Construction of the complex began in 1956 to support the U.S. Air Force Thor Missile program. In 1957, 550 Thors were launched for testing before the system's eventual deployment. In the late 1960s NASA took over the facility and began launching the Delta rocket, a new three-stage space launch vehicle derived by McDonnell Douglas from the Thor.

The first Delta launch was in 1960, and the McDonnell Douglas team is using the Deltas for boosting commercial and scientific satellites into orbit for NASA. Over the years Delta has earned the nickname of "the workhorse" of NASA's rocket fleet, compiling an unequaled success rate. Over the past 10 years, which includes 47 launches, the team has achieved a 98-percent success rate.

Today the facility is ready to begin a new era of Delta operations. With the U.S. government's decision in 1986 to use the Delta to help reduce the backlog of shuttle payloads, there are now plans to launch up to 30 more Deltas. These include Deltas for NASA and new Delta IIs for the U.S. Air Force and for commercial customers.

The Delta team today is a streamlined, experienced crew numbering approximately 200, who occupy the launch pad facilities and a complex of buildings for management, engineering, and manufacturing.

In 1966 a separate McDonnell Douglas ordnance facility was established just south of Titusville. This plant was built to manufacture anti-armor missiles; its first product was the Dragon weapon system. This facility, recently renamed MDAC-Florida Missile Production, continues to make infantry assault weapons, the Tomahawk cruise missile, and various aircraft assemblies.

Today as always before, McDonnell Douglas Astronautics Company is an integral part of the American space program, and as such continues to have a tremendous economic and historic impact on the recent history of Brevard County.

The McDonnell Douglas Delta 180 lifts off from Complex 17 on the Cape Canaveral Air Force Station at 11:08 a.m. September 5, 1986.

HOLIDAY INN COCOA BEACH

Ensconced next to the Atlantic Ocean in the heart of Cocoa Beach lies the Holiday Inn. This favorite spot of tourists, business people, and locals is a far cry from the miniscule property that opened its doors for business in December 1959.

That year the Holiday Inn had only 99 rooms. It was opened as a franchise to fulfill a need: The space program was just getting under way, and motel rooms in the area were at a premium.

As Cocoa Beach and all of Brevard County grew, so did the Holiday Inn Cocoa Beach. This was a time when astronauts were everywhere and were recognized when they made their way around the county. The housing industry and retail establishments had trouble keeping up with the sudden growth. And through it all the Holiday Inn Cocoa Beach was there.

In 1960 the Holiday Inn Cocoa Beach gave up its franchise status and became a part of Holiday Inn, Inc. By 1963 it was necessary to add 75 more rooms in what is now called the Promenade Watch building. At the time the Ramada Inn opened up next door—the building eventually became the executive offices in the Holiday Inn Cocoa Beach complex. By 1973 the Parkside building had been added, providing an additional 84 rooms. The property continued to expand, responding to the ever-increasing demand for rooms as Brevard County boomed.

In 1979 the Surfside building

Above: The Holiday Inn Cocoa Beach opened in 1959 with 99 rooms. It now has 500 guest rooms plus convention and dining facilities.

Below: The Holiday Inn Cocoa Beach has a large outdoor pool for those who prefer a leisurely swim.

Visitors may stroll the lushly landscaped promenade areas and enjoy the sea breezes, or take advantage of the hotel's many recreational facilities.

was completed, and the inn was enjoying an extremely high occupancy rate. But there still were no banquet facilities, which were needed to keep pace with the county's growth and evolution.

Brevard County grew rapidly, and the hotel was updated many times to accommodate the increase in business and tourist trade in the area.

In 1980 the Holiday Inn Cocoa Beach acquired the Beach Side Motel, which was just south of the complex, from owner Frank Wolfe. Wolfe had started a tradition in the lounge—the famous Cocoa Beach Jazz Festival—on Labor Day weekends. Today the jazz festival continues under the auspices of the Holiday Inn Cocoa Beach. Renovations on the Beach Side Motel made possible the conversion of 20 guest rooms into the current banquet and executive office facilities. After this project was completed, Holiday Lane was laid out. It includes the Promenade Walk, beach observation deck, and recreation facilities.

In 1983 the architecturally beautiful present complex was completed, boasting a total of 500 guest rooms, including 13 two-room beach-view suites, 18 bilevel lofts, 16 villa apartments, and banquet facilities that can accommodate 15 to 475 people—not bad for a hotel that started out with 40 employees and now has more than 250.

In 1988 the Holiday Inn Cocoa Beach and several other Holiday Inn properties were purchased by Holiday Inns International.

The Holiday Inn Cocoa Beach is a shining example of how the tourist and resort industry has expanded in Brevard County. Not only did the scope of the complex enlarge by a whopping 400 percent, the architectural aesthetics were addressed as well. The Holiday Inn Cocoa Beach is a refreshing example of how growth, when approached properly with the right balance and considerations, can enhance a property's value and please everyone. Today the Holiday Inn Cocoa Beach is a classically beautiful testimonial to the overall business expansion in Brevard County that was created along the way as the county and the inn reached maturation.

CLIFTON CONSTRUCTION

The Clifton family goes back six generations in Brevard and Volusia counties. One of Bob Clifton's ancestors was the first lighthouse keeper at Cape Canaveral.

Bob can remember in 1947 riding with Game Warden L.A. Tyndall through the Cape Canaveral area and seeing moonshine stills. There was an unwritten agreement between game wardens and moonshiners that when a game warden saw a still he would not report it in return for the moonshiners not shooting at the game wardens.

Clifton Construction was formally incorporated in 1961, although its actual beginning dates back to 1948, when Bob Clifton started working for his father as a mason's tender. Bob Clifton left in 1951 to get his degree at the University of Florida and to do a tour as a pilot in the Air Force. In 1961 he returned to the construction business his father had started and incorporated it as Clifton Construction.

That same year most of the contractors in Brevard County had dealt with the initial building boom and, finding a shortage of work, had gone out of business. The demise of these early construction companies left Clifton Construction in the enviable position of being one of the oldest construction firms in Brevard County.

An avid flier even before his Air Force days, Bob Clifton remembers the Brevard County of the past with fondness. One of his favorite memories is landing his airplane on State Road 520, which in 1951 was not the throughway it is today. He used to keep his plane tied to the palmettos along the side of the road.

Clifton has never given up his love of flying, and it has brought him into contact with some interesting people. He often flew his biplane with Dick Scobee, the commander of the ill-fated Space Shuttle *Challenger*.

Clifton determined early on that the best way to survive in the construction business is to do quality building. He believes that his penchant for high quality is what has made his company so successful. He knew that he would be in Brevard County for the rest of his life and that his son, Mark, would live in the county too and take over the firm at some point. He wanted to establish a reputation that would carry the company through his tutelage and that of his son. Mark Clifton is currently secretary/treasurer of Clifton Construction, and his father is looking to the day that he and Roger Patrick, vice-president, take over the reins.

Clifton Construction has built many well-known structures around Brevard County. One of the best known is the new Cocoa Beach Area Chamber of Commerce building on Fortenberry Road, Merritt Island. The company has built many manufacturing plants, including Cadillac Gage, Scientific Systems, Reflectone Corp., Ensco Inc., Fairchild Test Systems, and Sealy Mattress. Clifton Construction is also responsible for four beautiful Brevard County shopping areas: Rockledge Square, Port St. John Square, Banana River Square in Cocoa Beach, and Windover Square in Melbourne. Another well-known Clifton structure is the High Point Office Building in Cocoa.

When the company was first incorporated, there were only two employees, and that year, 1961, Clifton Construction did approximately $250,000 in business. In the past few years Clifton Construction employed slightly fewer than 100 people and did $17 million in business.

Clifton Construction's office staff in 1988.

In the early 1900s, the coastline of Brevard was an ideal location for scenic afternoon drives. Courtesy, Al and Bernice Stefurak

PATRONS

The following individuals, companies, and organizations have made a valuable commitment to the quality of this publication. Windsor Publications and the Cocoa Beach Area Chamber of Commerce gratefully acknowledge their participation in *Brevard County: From Cape of the Canes to Space Coast*.

W.S. Black Company, Inc.*
Canaveral Port Authority*
Clifton Construction*
Davies & Houser*
DBA Systems, Inc.*
Fat Boys' Franchise Systems, Inc.*
Florida Institute of Technology*
FLORIDA TODAY*
Grumman Corporation*
Holiday Inn Cocoa Beach*
KMD Ship Repair*
McDonnell Douglas Astronautics
  Company*
Mid-Florida Freezers*
Morton Thiokol, Inc.*
Port Canaveral*
Port Canaveral Towing Inc.*
Premier Cruise Lines, Ltd.*
Jim Rathmann Chevrolet-Cadillac, Inc.*
Ron Jon Surf Shop*
SeaEscape Limited*
Wuesthoff Health Systems, Inc.*

*Partners in Progress of *Brevard County: From Cape of the Canes to Space Coast*. The histories of these companies and organizations appear in Chapter Seven, beginning on page 97.

The Cocoa City Dock, shown here in the 1920s, was one of many piers which provided a central and exciting aspect of life in Brevard County. Courtesy, Al and Bernice Stefurak

Many a sunny afternoon was spent fishing off the docks in Brevard County. Al Trail and his wife are pictured here in the early 1920s on the Cocoa-Merritt Island Bridge. Courtesy, Al and Bernice Stefurak

BIBLIOGRAPHY

Astronauts themselves. *We Seven.* New York: Simon and Schuster, 1962.

Barbour, Thomas. *That Vanishing Eden.* New York: Little, 1944.

Barrientes, Bartolome. *Pedro Menendez de Aviles.* Gainesville: University of Florida Press, 1965.

Bartram, William. *The Travels of William Bartram.* Edited by Francis Harper. New Haven: Yale University Press, 1958.

Battle, Ethel Wilson. *Memories of the Early Days of Titusville.* Titusville: Unpublished.

Bennett, Charles E. *The Settlement of Florida.* Gainesville: The University of Florida Press, 1969.

―――. *Southernmost Battlefields of the Revolution.* Virginia: Blair, 1970.

Bowe, Richard J. *Pictorial History of Florida.* Tallahassee: 1965.

Brevard County, Florida Comprehensive Impact Fee Study. Tampa: 1987.

Brevard Economic Development Council. *Directory of Manufacturing and Related Industries, Brevard County, Florida.* Cocoa, Florida: 1987.

Caidin, Martin. *Spaceport U.S.A.* New York: Dutton, 1959.

Caron, Eric C. *One Hundred Years of Rockledge: Brevard's Oldest City.* Dallas: Taylor and Co., 1986.

Carr, Harriet. *Cape Canaveral-Cape of Storms and Wild Cane Fields.* St. Petersburg, Florida: Valkyrie Press, 1974.

Cocoa Beach Area Chamber of Commerce. *A Tourist Guide for the Cocoa Beach Area.* See Publications, 1987.

Corse, Carita Doggett. *Dr. Andrew Turnbull and the New Smyrna Colony in Florida.* St. Petersburg, Florida: The Great Outdoors Publishing, 1967.

Couch, Ernie. *Florida Trivia.* Tennessee: Rutledge Hill Press 1986.

Cummings, Betty Sue. *Let a River Be.* New York: Atheneum, 1978.

―――. *Say These Names, Remember Them.* Englewood, Florida: Pineapple Press, 1984.

Cushman, Joseph D. *A Goodly Heritage, The Episcopal Church in Florida: 1821-1892.* Gainesville: University of Florida Press, 1965.

Davis, W.W. *The Civil War and Reconstruction in Florida.* Gainesville: University of Florida Press, 1964.

De Holguin, Beatrice. *Tales of Palm Beach.* New York: Vantage Press, 1968.

Department of Community Relations of Holmes Regional Medical Center. *Fifty Years of Service; A History of Health Care Services in South Brevard.* Melbourne: 1982.

Fairbanks, Charles H. *Ethnohistorical Report on the Florida Indians.* New York: Garland Publishing Inc., 1974.

Fairbanks, George R. *The History of Florida.* Philadelphia: 1871.

Fontaneda. *Memoire Respecting Florida.* 1575. Revised 1944.

Gannon, Michael V. *The Cross in the Sand.* Gainesville: The University of Florida Press, 1965.

Geiger, Maynard. *The Franciscan Conquest of Florida.* Washington: 1936.

Gill, Joan E., ed. *Born of the Sun.* Hollywood, Florida: Bicentennial, 1975.

Hanna, A.J. *Lake Okeechobee.* New York: Bobbs-Merrill, 1948.

Hicks, John. *Zora Neale Hurston, A Portrait.* Orlando Sentinel Star, 1978.

Hicks, Miriam K. and Eleanor Schlatter. *The Mission of St. John's Episcopal Church, Eau Gallie, Florida.* Melbourne: Yates Publishing Company, 1981.

Hoag, Amey R. *Thy Lighted Lamp, a History of Holy Trinity Episcopal Church, Melbourne, Florida.* Melbourne: Undersea Press, 1958.

Hole, Louis J. *Melbourne Sketches, A Souvenir of Melbourne on the Indian River.* Melbourne: Brevard Graphics, 1975; originally published 1895.

Hoole, W. Stanley. *The Diary of Master Edward Clifford Anderson.* USN, University of Alabama Press, 1976.

Hopwood, Fred A. *Steamboating on the Indian River.* Melbourne, Florida: Self Published, 1985.

―――. *A History of West Melbourne.* Melbourne, Florida: Self Published, 1984.

Horton, Jack B. *Titusville, The First 60 Years.* Privately printed, 1960.

―――. *The Episcopal Church in Titusville, 1869-1987.* Privately printed, 1987.

Hurston, Zora Neale. *Dust Tracks on a Road.* New York: Arno, 1969.

Information Research Services. *Working and Living in the Cape Kennedy Area.* Webster Association, 1969.

Institute for Social Research. *NASA Impact on Brevard County.* Tallahassee, Florida: State University Press, 1966.

Jenkins, Sara. *Saddlebag Parsons.* New York: Thomas Y. Crowell, 1956.

Johns, June, ed. *Brevard County Relocation Guide.* Birmingham, Michigan: Exclusive Publications, 1987.

Kellersberger, Julia Lake. *Rooted in Florida Soil.* Melbourne, Florida: FIT Press, 1971.

Kelly, Dr. Fred. *America's Astronauts and Their Indestructible Spirit*. Blue Ridge Summit, Pennsylvania: Aero, a division of TAB Books, Inc., 1986.

Kendrick, Baynard. *Florida's Trails to Turnpikes, 1914-1964*. Gainesville: University of Florida Press, 1964.

Kersey, Harry A. *Pelts, Plumes and Hides; White Traders Among the Seminoles; 1780-1830*. Gainesville, Florida: University of Florida Press, 1975.

Kjerulff, Georgianna. *Tales of Old Brevard*. Melbourne: South Brevard Historical Society, 1972.

———. *The Hernandez-Capron Trail*. Unpublished.

———. *Troubled Paradise: The Story of Melbourne Village*. Melbourne: Kellersbuger Foundation, 1988.

Kornberg, Patti. *But It Is In Brevard*. Orlando: Daniels Publishing Company, 1982.

Landfried, James E. *So You're Coming to Disney World*. Melbourne, Florida: Islands Unlimited, 1972.

Laudonniere, Rene. *Three Voyages*. Translated by Charles E. Bennett. Gainesville: University of Florida Press, 1975.

Lewis, Richard S. *Challenger: The Final Voyage*. New York: Columbia University Press, 1988.

Martin, Robert H. *From These Beginnings, A History of St. Mark's Episcopal Church, Cocoa*.

Marx, Robert F. *The Treasure Fleets of the Spanish Main*. New York: World Publishing Company, 1968.

McKemy, Noreda and Weona Cleveland. *Melbourne, A Century of Memories*. Melbourne Centennial Commission, 1980.

Media, Southwestern Bell. *The Space Coast Welcomes You to Patrick Air Force Base*. San Diego, California: Blake Publishing Company, 1987.

News and Feature Articles in *Florida Today; Melbourne Times; Cocoa Tribune; Eau Gallie Journal; Orlando Sentinel; National Geographic Magazine*.

Neyland, Leedell. *Twelve Black Floridians*. Tallahassee, Florida: Florida A&M Press, 1970.

Nolan, David. *Fifty Feet in Paradise: The Booming of Florida*. New York: Harcourt, Brace, Jovanavich, 1984.

Orange County Bicentennial Commission. *More Than a Memory*. Orlando, 1976.

Panagopoulos, E.P. *New Smyrna*. Gainesville: University of Florida Press, 1966.

Pan-American World Services, Inc. *From Sand to Moondust*. Patrick Air Force Base: 1972.

Pareja, Francisco. *1613 Confessionario*. Edited by Jerald T. Milanich. Tallahassee: Division of Archives, History and Records Management, 1972.

Patrick, Rembert W. *Florida Under Five Flags*. Gainesville: University of Florida Press, 1945.

Pratt, Theodore. *Seminole*. New York: Duell, Sloan and Pearce, 1954.

Rabac, Glenn. *The City of Cocoa Beach, The First Sixty Years*. Winona, Minnesota: Apollo Books, 1986.

Ribault, Jean. *The Whole and True Discovery of Terra Florida*. London: 1563.

Roberts, William. *An Account of the First Discovery, and Natural History of Florida, 1763*. Facsimile Edition. Gainesville: University of Florida Press, 1976.

Scarboro, C.W. *Arrow at America's Spaceport*. Little Rock, Arkansas: Pioneer Press, 1966.

Schuster, Margery A. *Georgianna United Methodist Church, 1886-1986*. Privately printed, 1987.

Simmons, William Hayne. *Notices of East Florida*. Facsimile of 1822 Edition. Gainesville: University of Florida Press, 1973.

Smiley, Nixon. *Yesterday's Florida*. Miami: A. Seemann, 1974.

Smith, Julian Floyd. *Slavery and Plantation Growth in Antebellum Florida, 1821-1860*. Gainesville: University of Florida Press, 1973.

Smith, Mary Ellen (Mike). *Florida; A Way of Life*. New York: Dutton, 1959.

Smith, Patrick D. *A Land Remembered*. Englewood, Florida: Pineapple Press, 1984.

Starling, Merry Lynn, ed. *Caring, Sharing and Growing, Wuesthoff Hospital Inc., Annual Report*. Rockledge: 1986.

Starr, J. Barton. *Tories, Dons and Rebels; East Florida in the American Revolution*. Cooper Press, 1949.

Stone, Elaine Murray. *The Melbourne BiCentennial Book*. Melbourne: Brevard Graphics, 1976.

———. *Gateway to the Moon*. Unpublished, 1971.

———. *Pedro Menendez de Aviles, and the Founding of St. Augustine*. New York: P.J. Kenedy and Sons, 1969.

Stuart, Hix C. *The Notorious Ashley Gang*. Stuart, Florida: St. Lucie Printing Co., 1928.

Taylor, L.B. *Lift Off: The Story of America's Spaceport*. New York: Dutton, 1968.

Tebeau, Charlton W. *A History of Florida*. Coral Gables: University of Miami Press, 1971.

Thomas, Frank J. *Early Days in Melbourne Beach, 1888-1928*. Cocoa Beach, Florida: Jet Press, 1968.

———. *Melbourne Beach, The First One Hundred Years*. Melbourne: Centennial Commission, 1983.

Thrift, Charles T., Jr. *The Trail of the Florida Circuit Rider*. Lakeland: Florida Southern College Press, 1944.

Thurm, Ann H. *The History of the City of Cape Canaveral*. Privately printed, 1987.

Van Atta, Marian. *Living Off The Land*. Cocoa, Florida: Self Published, 1973.

Wagner, Kip. *Pieces of Eight*. New York: E.P. Dutton, 1966.

Weggs, Wanton S. *History of Florida*. 1885. Republished in *Titusville Star-Advocate*, 1955.

Wolfe, Tom. *The Right Stuff*. New York: Farrar, Straus & Giroux, 1979.

INDEX

Partners in Progress Index

Black Company, Inc., W.S., 115
Canaveral Port Authority, 104-106
Clifton Construction, 126
Cocoa Beach Area Chamber of Commerce, 98
Davies & Houser, 102
DBA Systems, Inc., 103
Fat Boys' Franchise Systems, Inc., 114
Florida Institute of Technology, 121
FLORIDA TODAY, 99
Grumman Corporation, 119
Holiday Inn Cocoa Beach, 124-125
KMD Ship Repair, 110
McDonnell Douglas Astronautics Company, 122-123
Mid-Florida Freezers, 113
Morton Thiokol, Inc., 116-117
Port Canaveral, 112
Port Canaveral Towing Inc., 111
Premier Cruise Lines, Ltd., 108-109
Rathmann Chevrolet-Cadillac, Inc., Jim, 118
Ron Jon Surf Shop, 100-101
SeaEscape Limited, 107
Wuesthoff Health Systems, Inc., 120

General Index
Italicized numbers indicate illustrations.

Abbott, Karl P., 43
African Village, Johnny Weismuller's, 70
Aikens, Linwood B., 36, *37*
Airports: 44; Dunn, 21; Melbourne, 44, 51, 65, 82, 85; Spaceport Executive, 83
Aldrin, Edwin E., *72*, *73*
Allen, Balaam, 29
American Revolution, 16
Anders, Bill, 71
Andrews, R.N., 27
Archaeological sites, *10*, *11*, *12*, *15*
Armstrong, Neil A., 65, *72*, *73*
Art exhibitions and competitions, 82
Arts and culture, 82
Aspinwall, John, 28

Bahama Beach Club, 43, 51, 57. *See also* Indialantic Casino
Ballard, S. Thruston, 41; estate of, *41*
Banana River Naval Air Station, 50, 51, 52, 53, 54, 55
Baseball, 84
Bean, I.F., 47
Bergin, J.F., 33

Bertsch, Willem, 82
Blacks, 29, 42, 67, 73
Bluford, Guion, 85
Boardman, Lucy H., 30
Borman, Frank, 71
Borsodi, Ralph, 54, 55
Bourinot, Harry, 45
Boyd, Joseph, 66
Boyer, Alex, 78
Brady, E.L., 21
Brevard, Theodore Washington, 9
Brevard Arts Council, 82
Brevard County School Board, 67
Brevard Hospital Association, 47
Brevard Hospital Service Guild, 54
Brevard Regional Arts Group, 82
Brevard Symphony Orchestra, 64, 66, 82
Brothers, John, 42, 67
Brothers, Mary, 42
Brothers, William Rufus, 42
Brothers, Wright, 29, 30, 38, 42
Brown, B. Frank, 64
Brown, William M., 23
Burnham, Mills Olcutt, 20, 21, 22, 28
Burns, Haydon, 56

Campbell, Charles F., 30
Canaveral Club, 36
Canaveral National Seashore, *10*, 78
Canaveral Press Club, 84
Cape Canaveral (the Cape), 12, 13, 14, 16, 20, 21, 31, 45, 52, 56, 59, 63, 65, 69, 72, 76, 81
Cape Canaveral (city), 59, 70, 88
Cape Canaveral Air Force Station, 48, 62, 63, 64, 65, 66, 68, 69, 72, 76, 77, 86, 88
Cape Canaveral Fire Department, 58
Cape Canaveral Lighthouse, 48
Cape Canaveral Pier, Old, *58*
Cape Kennedy, 65
Carlile, David Nathaniel, 21
Carlile, Lawrence, 21
Carpenter, Scott, 62, 64
Castleman, John B., 39, 41
Cattle ranching, 37
Centennial celebrations, 87
Center for the Performing Arts, 82
Cernan, Eugene A., *60*, 74
Chaffee, Roger, *71*
Churches: Allen Chapel AME, 42; Community Chapel, 52; Congregational, 30; First Baptist (Eau Gallie), 28; First Baptist (Merritt Island), 58; First Georgianna, *91*; First Methodist (Melbourne), 30, 32; First Methodist (Titusville), 39; Holy Trinity Episcopal, 30, 78, 87; Melbourne Beach Community Chapel, 33; Rockledge Presbyterian, 26; St. David's By-the-Sea Episcopal, 63; St. Gabriel's Episcopal, 22, 30, 87; St. John's Episcopal, 28; St. Joseph's Catholic, 39, 87; St. Luke's Episcopal, 23; St. Mark's Episcopal, 26, 30, 47; St. Mary's, 31; St. Paul's, 31; St. Paul's Methodist, 40
Cities, towns, and communities: Cape Canaveral, 12, 13, 14, 16, 20, 21, 31, 45, 52, 56, 59, 62, 63, 64, 65, 66, 68, 69, 70, 72, 76, 81, 88; Cocoa, 17, 23, 24, 26, 27, 29, 30, 37, 40, 42, 44, 45, 46, 47, *53*, 56, 57, 66, 67, 68, 70, 71, 73, 76, 78, 79, 81, 82, 84, 87, 93; Cocoa Beach, 23, 45, 46, 50, 52, 55, 56, 57, 62, 63, 64, 68, 72, 78, 79, 83, 84, 86, 87, 88, *94*; Courtenay, 23; Deer Park, 38; Eau Gallie, 12, 22, 27, 28, 32, 36, 39, 40, 41, 42, 43, 47, 50, 52, 54, 56, 68, 71, 78, 82; Enterprise, 17, 27, 35; Georgiana, 23, 24; Grant, 83; Hopkins, 38, 40; Indialantic, 21, 42, 43, 53, 56, 57, 77, 79, 84, 86; Indian Harbour Beach, 12, 43, 57, 58, 63, 83, 95; LaGrange, 20, 21; Melbourne, 17, 24, 27, 29-33, 36, 37, 38, 40, 41, 42, 43, 44, 47, 49, 52, 56, 57, 64, 66, 67, 68, 76, 84, 86, 87; Melbourne Beach, 32, 33, 50, 53, 82, 86; Merritt Island, 10, 12, *14*, 20, 23, 32, 36, 42, 43, 45, 53, 58, 69, 71, 72, 77, 79, 80, 82, 91, 92, 93; Micco, 37; Mims, 21; Palm Bay, 33, 39, 66, 76, 78, 86, 87; Pineda, 38; Port St. John, 79; Rockledge, 18, 22, 24, 26, 31, 36, 39, 41, 44, 45, 46, 47, 67, 68, 78, 79, 87, 93; Sand Point, 20, 21, 22, 23; Satellite Beach, 57, 64, 70, 86; Scottsmoor, 82; Sharpes, 87; South Melbourne, 29, 67, 78; South Merritt Island, 58; South Titusville, 79; Tillman, 33, 39; Titusville, 10, 11, 16, 17, 21, 22, 23, 24, 30, 34, 35, 36, 37, *39*, 40, 41, 46, 47, 51, 53, *54*, 56, 66, 68, 69, 70, 72, 76, 79, 80, 83, 84, 86, 87, 88; Valkaria, 51; West Melbourne, 37, 82; Whispering Hills, 68
Citrus growing, 20, 24, 37
Civil War, 21, 24, 27, 28, 37, 41, 45

Cocoa, 17, 23, 24, 26, 27, 29, 30, 37, 40, 42, 44, 45, 46, 47, 53, 56, 57, 66, 67, 68, 70, 71, 73, 76, 78, 79, 81, 82, 84, 87, 93; business district, 27; churches, 26, 30, 47; colleges, 66, 81; hotels, 26, 27; newspapers, 27, 45; schools, 66, 67; theaters, 40; yacht club, 26
Cocoa Beach, 23, 45, 46, 50, 52, 55, 56, 57, 62, 63, 64, 68, 72, 78, 79, 83, 84, 86, 87, 88, 94; churches, 52, 63; hotels and motels, 56, 64, 86; theaters, 63
Cocoa Isles, 56
Cocoa-Merritt Island Bridge, 23, 27
Cocoa-Rockledge Land Company, 45
Cocoa-Rockledge Railroad Station, 36
Cocoa State Bank, 26
Cocoa Village Playhouse, 40
Colleges and universities: Brevard Community College, 66, 81, 82; Brevard Engineering College, 51, 55; Brevard Junior College, 66; Florida Agricultural College, 28; Florida Institute of Technology, 40, 51, 55, 66, 83, 86, 121; Florida State University, 11; Melbourne University, 55; Shelton Bible College, 67; University of Florida, Gainesville, 28
Collins, Michael, 72
Communications, 22-23, 37, 68
Conrad, Charles, Jr., 77
Cooper, G.V., 46
Cooper, Gordon, 62, 65
Coschutt, Tom, 21
Couch, Roy O., 53, 54
County seat, selection of, 22
Courtenay, 23
Crane Creek, 29, 30, 32, 38, 40, 47
Creel, W.J., 42
Crippen, Robert, 80, 81
Crystal Ice Company, 36
Cunningham, Walter, 71
Curley, Michael J., 31

Daniel, Josephine, 26
Daniel, L.S., 26
Debus, Kurt, 63
Deer Park, 38
Delannoy, John, 26
Delannoy, Sarah, 26
Denius, Homer, 65
Denius, Marcia, 82
Depression, Great, 30, 44, 46
Disney World, 76
Drought of 1982, 84
Dummit, Douglas, 20, 22
Dummit, Thomas, 20
Duncan, Lydia, 42

Earle, Herbert R., 43
East Coast Lumber, 52

Eastern Space and Missile Center, 88
Eau Gallie, 12, 22, 27, 28, 32, 36, 39, 40, 41, 42, 43, 47, 50, 52, 54, 56, 68, 71, 78, 82; boat works, 39; churches, 28, 40; hotels, 28, 43; Hyde Park, 39; schools, 39, 40, 67; Sunset Terrace, 50; theaters, 40; yacht club, 39, 57
Edwards, Gus, 45, 46
Eisele, Don, 71
Elbow Creek, 41
Ensemble Theatre, 82
Enterprise, 17, 27, 35
Entertainment, 40-41, 45, 51, 83
Environmental groups, 78
Evans, Ronald E., 74
Exploration, 12-15

Feaster, Andrew, 21
Fee, William, 32
Festivals, 83
Fishing industry, 58
Flagler, Henry, 33, 36, 39
Florida, statehood of, 21
Florida Space Coast Philharmonic, 82
Forts: Ann, 17, 20; Caroline, 13; Dallas, 17; Gatlin, 17; Lauderdale, 17; Pierce, 17, 19, 31, 42; San Marcos, 13; Taylor, 17
Fortune 500 corporations, 88
Friedland, Nathan, 67

Gannett Plaza, 68
Geologic history, 10
Georgiana, 23, 24
Gibson, Andrew, 23
Gibson, U.F., 67
Gingras, Gabriel, 27, 30, 31
Gingras, George, 27
Gleason, Lansing, 57
Gleason, William H., 28
Glenn, John, 62, 63
Golf, 83
Goode, Alexander John, 52
Goode, Jessie, 29, 30
Goode, John, 40
Goode, Richard, 29, 30, 40
Grabel, R.E., 46
Grant, 83
Graves, Cyrus E., 32, 33
Greater South Brevard Area Chamber of Commerce, 86
Grissom, Virgil "Gus," 62, 63, 65, 71
Gunthrope, Lucy, 82

Haisten, James A., Sr., 46
Harbour Isles, 57
Hardee, Gardner, 24, 26, 36
Harding, Warren D., 45
Hargrave, William, 47
Harmon, S.W., 22
Harris, Anneda, 42

Harris Corporation, 51, 66
Harrison, John, 21
Hartley, John T., 66
Hay, Isaac M., 47
Hay, Lucille, 47
Hector, Cornthwaite John, 29
Hedgecock, Percy L., 57
Hicks, I.K., 47
Hipp, Gus, 79
Historic buildings, 87
Hodgson, Alexander, 39
Hodgson brothers, 28
Hopkins, George, 37-38
Hopkins, 38, 40
Hospitals: 87; Brevard, 56, 67, 78; Cape Canaveral, 64, 78, 87; Community Psychiatric, 87; Devereux Children's, 87; Florida East Coast, 47; Holmes Regional Medical Center, 82; Patrick Air Force Base, 88; Sea Pines Rehabilitation, 87; Wuesthoff, 45, 47, 56, 78, 87
Hotels: 86; Airport Hilton, 86; Bellevue, 32; Brevard, 26, 78; Brown, 33; Cape Canaveral Hilton, 67; Cape Colony Motel, 64; Carleton, 32-33; Cocoa Beach Hilton, 86; Cocoa House, 27; Colonial Inn, 56; Crenshaw, 47; Delmonico, 27; Goode House, 30; Granada, 28; Harbor City, 43; Holiday Inn, 64, 87, 124-125; Hotel Dixie, 22, 34; Howard Johnson's, 64; Imperial, 43; Indialantic, 43, 44, 45; Indian River, 24, 26, 45; Lund House, 22; Melbourne Beach Hilton, 86; Melbourne Hilton, 86; Neptune Hall, 53; Oaks, 24; Oleanders, 43, 56; Plaza, 24, 26; Radisson, 86; Ramada Inn, 64, 86, 87; River House, 43; Royal Poinciana, 36; Starlite Motel, 56, 62, 63; Titus House, 22; Trade Winds, 43, 44, 45, 56; Villa Marine, 32
House of 1916, 83
Houston, John C., 27, 28, 88; residence of, 28
Houston, Mary Virginia, 27
Howard Johnson Plaza, 86
Huchinson, Margaret, 54
Hughlett, Nannie Wilkinson, 26
Hughlett, William Leland, 26
Hughlett Drug Company, 26
Humphrey, Hubert H., 70, 71
Hurricanes, 14, 45, 46, 54, 84
Hurston, Zora Neale, 42

Indialantic, 21, 42, 43, 53, 56, 57, 77, 79, 84, 86; hotels, 43, 53, 86; Trade Winds Club, 57
Indialantic Casino, 43. *See also* Bahama Beach Club

Indian Harbour Beach, 12, 43, 57, 58, 63, 83, 95; schools, 57
Indianola Cemetery, 23
Indian River Bank, 23
Indian River Catholic Colony, 39
Indian River County, 30, 85
Indian River Yacht Club, 26
Indians: Ais, 12, 13, 14; Creek, 14, 15; Jeaga, 13, 14; Seminole, 8, 15, 16, 17, 20, 90
Integration of schools, 67

Jackson, Estella, 42
Jackson, Henry, 67
Jetty Park, 16, 59
Johnson, Lyndon, 63, 65, 72
Jones, Johnny, 93
Jupiter, 22, 36

Kenaston, Tom, 47
Kennedy, John F., 64, 65, 66, 73
Kennedy Space Center, 68, 69, 71, 73, 74, 77, 79, 80, 81, 84, 85, 86; press corps of, 84
Kerwin, Joseph P., 77
Keuper, Jerome, 55
King, Mercer Livermore, 56
Kling, Clifford B., 45
Kouwen-Hoven, Ernest, 42-43
Ku Klux Klan, 67

LaGrange, 20, 21
Lakes: Monroe, 17; Okeechobee, 8; Poinsett, 24, 56; Washington, 16, 84; Winder, 17
Lansing Beach, 52
LaRoche, James, 23
Lawrence, Harry, 42
Lovell, James, 71
Luffman, Shubel G., 20
Lumber industry, 37-38

McIntire, Carl, 67
McKeown, Arthur, 18, 24, 25
Magruder, Charles, 24
Magruder, Cornelia B., 26
Markou, Kypros, 82
Marshall, Joseph, 20
Martin, Stewart, 23
Marx, Jennifer, 82
Mason, Thomas, 29
Mathers, John, 43
Melbourne, 17, 24, 27, 29-33, 36, 37, 38, 40, 41, 42, 43, 44, 47, 49, 52, 56, 57, 64, 66, 67, 68, 76, 84, 86, 87; blacks, 42; churches, 30, 32, 42; clubs, 41, 67; colleges, 66; festivals, 83; hospitals, 47, 67; hotels, 30, 32-33, 47, 56, 86; library, 30; malls, 84; newspapers, 37, 67; police department, 82; schools, 40, 42, 64, 67; yacht club, 33

Melbourne Air Station, 54
Melbourne Angler's Club, 41
Melbourne Band, 40
Melbourne Beach, 32, 33, 50, 53, 82, 86; boardinghouses, 32; churches, 33; hotels, 32
Melbourne Beach Casino, 40, 51
Melbourne Cemetery, 52
Melbourne Country Club, 67
Melbourne Harbor, 52
Melbourne Naval Air Station, 44, 51
Melbourne Square Mall, 84
Melbourne Village, 54, 55
Merritt Island, 10, 12, 14, 20, 23, 32, 36, 42, 43, 45, 53, 58, 69, 71, 72, 77, 79, 80, 82, 91, 92, 93; Banyan, 23; Brantley, 23; churches, 58, 91; Courtenay, 23; Georgianna, 23; Hacienda Del Sol, 43; Haulover area, 20; Indianola, 23; Lotus, 23; Tropic, 23
Merritt Square Mall, 79
Micco, 37
Mims, 21
Miracle City Mall, 69
Missions and missionaries, 13
Mobile home communities, 82
Morton, Rogers, 41
Morton, Thruston, 41
Mosquito County, 19
Mosquito Lagoon, 17
Mounds, shell, 12
Munson, Dell C., 24
Murkshe, Bob, 64
Museums: Air Force Museum, 81; Brevard Art Center and Museum, 82; Brevard Museum of History and Natural Science, 78, 82; McLarty Museum of Sunken Treasure, 83; Memorial Museum, 87

Nannie Lee's Strawberry Mansion, 78
NASA, 53, 59, 62, 64, 65, 69, 71, 72, 86
Nelson, Bill, 85
Nelson, Charles, 57
Neuharth, Allen H., 68
Nevins Fruit Company, 69
New Found Harbour, 58
New Smyrna Beach, 20
Newspapers: *Cocoa/Rockledge News*, 27; *Cocoa Tribune*, 45, 68; *East Coast Advocate*, 22; *Florida Star*, 22; *FLORIDA TODAY*, 68, 99; *Indian River Mirror*, 27; *Melbourne Times*, 37, 67; *Orlando Sentinel*, 68; *Star-Advocate*, 23; *Titusville Star*, 36; *TODAY*, 68; *USA TODAY*, 68
Nichols, Ted, 67
Norsk-Hydro Aluminum Works, 79
Nutting, Elizabeth, 54
Oaks, The, 84

Odiorne, Louise, 54
Osaki, Fred, 52
Osaki, Henry Y., 52
Oslin, Emmet D., 37

Palm Bay, 33, 39, 66, 76, 78, 86, 87; churches, 39; colleges, 66; population figures, 86; Port Malabar, 86
Parrish, Jesse, Jr., 69
Patrick Air Field, 64
Patrick Air Force Base, 50, 55, 56, 57, 62, 70, 71, 84, 88
Patterson, George F., 39
Payne's Landing, 20
Pineda, 38
Playalinda Beach, 46
Poor Richard's Inn, 32
Porcher, Byrnina Peck, 23, 27
Porcher, Edward, 23, 26
Port Canaveral, 58, 59, 80, 81, 84, 88, 94, 112; Jetty Park at, 16, 59
Port St. John, 79
Preston, G. Merritt, 63, 65
Pritchard, James, 23

Quality Court, 86

Radiation, Inc., 51, 65, 66
Railroads: Celestial, 36; Florida East Coast, 31, 36, 52; Jacksonville, Tampa, and Key West, 22; St. John's and Indian River, 36; Union Cypress, 38
Real Eight Company, 70
Real estate industry, 43, 44, 45, 56, 57
Reconstruction, 42
Recreation and leisure, 40, 43, 57, 81, 83, 89
Reddick, John, 21
Rehabilitation centers, 78
Rice, Clark, 22
Ride, Sally, 85
Riverfront Park, 51
River Isles, 56
Rivers: Banana, 6, 20, 45, 50, 57, 58, 71, 79, 83; Eau Gallie, 27, 28, 39; Indian, 10, 12, 17, 18, 20, 22, 23, 24, 26, 27, 28, 29, 32, 33, 35, 36, 41, 43, 44, 47, 50, 51, 54, 55, 57, 58, 70, 71, 78, 79, 83, 87, 88, 95; Mosquito, 10, 21; St. Johns, 12, 13, 15, 16, 17, 21, 24, 37, 83; St. Lucie, 10, 20
Rockledge, 18, 22, 24, 26, 31, 36, 39, 41, 44, 45, 46, 47, 67, 68, 78, 79, 87, 93; churches, 26, 31; golf and country club, 41; hospitals, 45, 47; hotels, 24, 26, 45; houses, 45, 93; Orange festival, 45; railroad station, 36, 37
Rockledge Landing, 24
Rossetter, James, Jr., 40

Rossetter, James Wadsworth, 41
Royal Oak Country Club, 69

Sailing competitions, 83
Sanders, Thomas, 23
Sand Point, 20, 21, 22, 23,
Satellite Beach 57, 64, 70, 86; hotels, 86; schools, 57
Schirra, Walter, 62, 64, 66, 71
Schmitt, Harrison H., 74
Schools: 23, 40; Astronaut High, 69; Central Catholic High, 66; Cocoa High, 66; Eau Gallie High, 67; Henegar, 82; Holy Trinity, 67; Kentucky Military Institute, 39; Melbourne High, 64, 83; Melbourne Vocational, 42; Ocean Breeze Elementary, 57; Our Lady of Lourdes, 67; St. Mark's, 67; Satellite High, 57; Stone High, 42, 67; Titusville Elementary, 96; Titusville High, 84
Scott, David R., 65
Scottsmoor, 82
Sears Town Mall, 69
Sebastian Beach Inn, 92
Sebastian Inlet, 50, 53, 54, 55, 70, 83, 87, 92
Segregation, 42, 67
Seminole Wars, 17, 20
Senior citizens housing, 78
Sharpes, 87
Shaw, George, 65
Shepard, Alan, 62, 63
Sherwood Country Club, 69
Shuster, Mary, 23
Slayton, Donald "Deke," 62
Smith, William Barton, 27
South Brevard Civic League, 42
South Brevard Historical Society, 82
South Brevard Junior League, 82
South Melbourne, 29, 67, 78
South Melbourne Beach, 52, 76
South Merritt Island, 58
South Titusville, 79
Space Coast Science Center, 82
Spaceport USA, 81, 86, 89
Space program, 56, 61-64, 68-69, 71-72, 74-75, 76-77, 79, 85-86
Space shuttles, 9, 36, 76, 77, 78, 79, 81, 85, 86, 88
Spanish-American War, 16
Spell, J.C., 46
Stewart, Arthur, 37
Stewart, Charles, 37
Stewart, Evelyn, 44
Stewart, W.T., 43
Stone Funeral Home, 42
Surfing, 83

Taylor, Albert Armer, 26
Taylor, Charles, 28
Taylor, Grace Webster, 26

Theaters, movie, 40
Tillman, John, 33
Tillman, 33, 39. See also Palm Bay
Titus, Henry T., 21, 22
Titus, Mary Evalina, 22
Titusville, 10, 11, 16, 17, 21, 22, 23, 24, 30, 34, 35, 36, 37, 39, 40, 41, 46, 47, 51, 53, 54, 56, 66, 68, 69, 70, 72, 76, 79, 80, 83, 84, 86, 87, 88; airports, 83; banks, 23; blacks, 23; churches, 22, 30, 39, 87; clubs, 36, 69, 86; colleges, 66; courthouse, 69; drugstore, 46; festivals, 83; fires, 37; freeze, 37; hotels, 22, 23, 34; malls, 69; Myers Cottage, 47; newspapers, 22, 23, 36; parks, 96; population, 69; Pritchard house, 23; railroad station, 36; schools, 40, 69, 84, 96; shopping centers, 69; shops, 22, 36
Tourism, 42, 52, 70, 76, 83
Trade Winds Club, 57
Trail, Al, 46
Trail, Maude E., 46
Transportation, 17, 32, 33, 35-36, 38, 44, 46, 53, 56, 70-71, 78-79, 85
Travis, S.F., 26
Treasure hunting, 14, 70
Truck farming, 37
Tucker Plumbing, 42
Tunicka, Maria, 82
Turkey Creek, 33
Turkey Creek Sanctuary, 78
Turpentine industry, 38
Turnbull, Andrew, 16; estate of, 20

Union Cypress Company, 39

Valentine, Amelia, 33
Valentine, May, 33
Valkaria, 51
Von Braun, Wernher, 64

Wager, Ellis, 41
Wager, P.E., 22
Wagner, Kip, 70
Warren, Joe, 23
Weitz, Paul J., 77
Wells, W.T., 30, 40
West Melbourne, 37, 82
Whispering Hills, 68
White, Ed, 71
White, Grady, 67
Whittfield, William, 24
Wilcox, Alfred, 32
Wildcat Yachting Club, 51
Wildlife preservation societies, 78
Wilkinson, J.N., 26
Willard, B.C., 26
Willard, B.S., 26
Willard, C.A., 26
Williams, Hiram Smith, 24, 87

Williams, Myra, 50
Wilson, Bruce, 66
Windover Farms, 10, 11, 15. See also Archaeological sites
Wood, Virginia, 54
World War I, 38, 40, 42, 44, 45, 46
World War II, 44, 47, 50-52, 53, 54, 55, 56, 83, 92
Wright, Peter, 29
Writers, 84
WWBC, 56

Young, John, 80, 81

Zies, Peter, 82